YOUR
NEXT STEPS

I0099347

(The Road To Successful
Christian Living)

Kenneth Sesley

YOUR NEXT STEPS

(The Road To Successful Christian Living)

by

Kenneth Sesley

Copyright © 2014 by Kenneth Sesley
All Rights Reserved.

Scripture verses quoted from The Holy Bible, New King James Version Copyright © 1982 by Thomas Nelson, Inc.

The New King James Bible, New Testament Copyright © 1979 by Thomas Nelson, Inc.

The New King James Bible, Old Testament Copyright © 1980 by Thomas Nelson, Inc.

Scripture taken from *The Message*. Copyright © 1993, 1994, 1995, 1996, 2000, 2001, 2002. Used by permission of NavPress Publishing Group."

Printed in the United States of America

Contents

Contents

Dedicated to:
All of you who are just beginning
(or re-beginning) your journey of faith.
May your trip to Calvary lead you to become a
fully developing disciple or followers of Jesus Christ!

Congratulations

The decision you've made to become a follower of Jesus Christ is the most important decision of your life. God created you with a purpose and that purpose begins with knowing Him. You may not be completely sure what happens next, now that you have decided to follow Jesus or what you should do now. There are probably a million questions running through your mind. This book will answer some of those questions and help you get on the right track in your new Christian life.

This means that anyone who belongs to Christ has become a new person. The old life is gone; a new life has begun! —2 Corinthians 5:17

Following Jesus is both a one-time decision and a life-long process. God wants you to have a meaningful life in relationship with Him through His Son, Jesus. However, he doesn't force that desire on you. He gives you a choice. You can choose to live according to His plan, or you can choose to go your own way. If you choose to say "no" to God—if you decide to live life on your own terms—that decision separates you from Him. Not only is refusing God a result of a sinful nature, it is sin itself.

On your own, there is nothing you can do to bring yourself into a right relationship with God. Good works won't do it. Religion won't do it. Morality won't do it. Neither will money nor philosophy nor knowledge nor science. For centuries, seekers have tried all of these paths with no success. As the image below portrays, there is a great chasm, gulf or fixed divide that seperates humanity from God...it is the sin gulf. There is nothing that we can do on our own to span or cross this gulf.

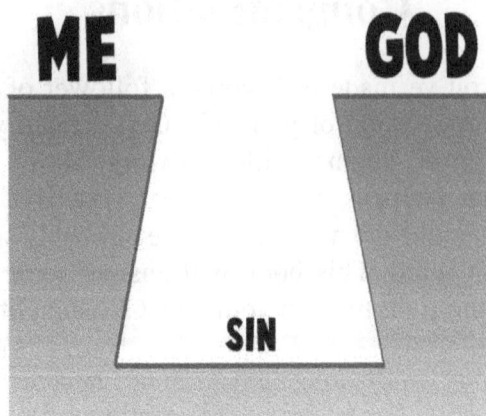

Take note of the story the following verses tell:

There is a path before each person that seems right, but it ends in death. Proverbs 14:12

But God showed his great love for us by sending Christ to die for us while we were still sinners. Romans 5:8

For there is only one God and one Mediator who can reconcile God and humanity—the man Christ Jesus. 1 Timothy 2:5

Christ suffered for our sins once for all time. He never sinned, but he died for sinners to bring you safely home to God. He suffered physical death, but he was raised to life in the Spirit. 1 Peter 3:18

As the image below shows, when you accepted, by faith, Jesus Christ's sacrificial and atoning work to remove the guilt and punishment for our sins at the Cross of Calvary, that divide between you and God was conquered by the power of His cross!

You took a big step by coming to the point of realization that Jesus is the only mediator who restores your relationship with God. You have prayed and asked Jesus to be the leader and director of your life. You've asked Him to forgive you for all the ways you've sinned against Him while living life on your own terms, and you've committed to becoming more like Him. At the

10

moment you asked Jesus to come into your life, He did. Your salvation is sealed and secure.

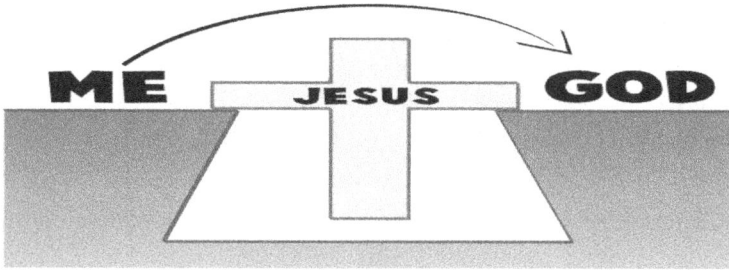

You can't "lose" your salvation, but the process of becoming a fully developing follower of Jesus Christ is ongoing. This is called discipleship.

There are tools to help you get started on this path— tools to help you better understand the decision you've made and to help you grow in your faith. In the following pages, you will find:

1. The story of how I became a follower of Jesus Christ;

2. An explanation of your six Next Steps;

3. Calvary Fellowship International's Statement of Beliefs;

4. The entire Gospel of John, plus a reading plan to help you get started;

5. And additional resources to help you grow.

The Bible says, "This means that anyone who belongs to Christ has become a new person. The old life is gone; a new life has begun!" (2 Cor. 5:17) If you have asked Jesus to forgive you of your sins and come into your life, then, according to God Himself, you are a new creation! As of right now, real life starts. Anything prior to knowing Jesus was simply *existing*, but knowing God and walking with Him is really *living*. Welcome to the Calvary, the family of God! —Pastor Kenneth Sesley

11

MY STORY...

My background is a little unusual. I was born in Los Angeles (not so unusual) to a single mother name Evelyn, who by the time I was two years old, was completely blind. Also, she was already 40 years old when I was born. There were two brothers and a sister before me. But they were 21½, 20 and nearly 15 years older than me. And, though my mother and I were poor by most people's standards, ours was a happy home.

But in addition to my mother's lack of sight, she was also a severe asthmatic. She was acutely aware of her failing health and so she raised me fairly strictly, because she always believed that she would die before I graduated from high school. Therefore momma wanted me to be able to take care of myself without becoming a burden on some other family member.

Now up till this time, I had a quasi-religious background. Most of my family were non-church going Southern Baptist, but I was mostly heathen. But occasionally I did attend church...usually on Easter. In fact, I had a Pentecostal Holiness godmother who would also take me to church. She would always make me pray what is known as the sinner's prayer afterwards. I really didn't mean it, but it was the only way to get her to stop sharing the gospel with me...just like going to church with her occasionally was the only way to get her to stop bugging me about going to church. She was a sweet old lady, but she was spooky. After becoming a Christian I grew to appreciate her commitment to Christ, but before then I really tried to steer clear of her. This continued for several years...but one day, either something that she said, or something that the minister said caught my attention and so when I prayed the sinner's prayer, this time, I meant it. I really felt like Christ had come into my heart. But I was what Black people used to call "mannish". This means that by eight or nine I could cuss with the best of them, fist fight and chased after girls. So when I told all my friends that I had gotten saved over the weekend, they all watched my behavior and when it didn't change, they kept trying to convince me that I wasn't really a Christian. And, because I wasn't a member of a church and had no mature Christian to help me understand what I am sharing with you, I believed them. So I really never thought that much about Christianity or being saved anymore.

12

Then one night, in January of 1976, all of my worst fears came true. I had a supernatural experience in which I had a series of dreams in which I kept seeing my mother experiencing cardiac arrest. She was in the hospital at the time, but she appeared to be improving in her health. There was nothing in my mind that would suspect what would occur that night. I began dreaming that my mother was experiencing numerous cardiac arrests. In the last scene of these series of dreams, I saw doctors around her using the paddles that they shock peoples hearts with. At some point, I also saw her lying there with her chest open and the doctors trying to manually get her heart going. Blood was everywhere.

Then, all of a sudden, the dream changed and she was lying on her bed dressed in all white! There was no blood, and no doctors. And in front of her bed stood this huge white winged being. Not Caucasian, but white like light. My mother was looking into his face and her face was shinning or glistening. I couldn't tell if it was the reflection from this being or whether the light was emanating from her. His wings were not extended, they were like an eagle's wings who had landed and was sitting still on a perch.

In addition to seeing my mother and this angel, I saw all of these wisps of clouds around the room. Then in the dream, she looked at me and said these words: "I'm gone", and with a gigantic swooshing sound the angel, my mother and these cloud like wisps all shot through the ceiling and I immediately woke up and sat straight up in my bed and looked at the clock. It was 3:00 a.m. Well I thought that I had just had a bad dream, so I lay back down and went back to sleep.

The next morning, I overslept. So I yelled to my sister (who was staying with my mother and me, along with her daughter, after a marital separation) that we had overslept and to wake my niece up for school. Then she came into my bedroom and as soon as I saw her face, I said: "Momma died last night didn't she!" Then we both just started crying and bawling.

On the day of my mother's funeral, the minister who did the "eulogy" quoted a Scripture from the Bible, saying: "The Lord giveth and the Lord taketh away...blessed be the name of the Lord". Then He went on to say that

13

God needed a beautiful flower for His heavenly garden, so He looked down here to earth and saw Evelyn and he plucked her from earth to plant her in His heavenly garden.

Instantly I thought: "If He's God, why didn't he make his own (expletive) flower". Then a hatred for God immediately took over my heart. Though I still believed in God I wanted nothing to do with Him; after all, according to the preacher, He had killed my mother and taken her from me. Today, I understand that this guy was speaking metaphorically, and actually trying to console our family, but it had the opposite affect on me. Once I would return to following Christ, I learned that this was a verse in the book of Job, but the man had misapplied the verse and taken it out of its context. It was truly stated in the Bible by Job, but it was a true statement. A careful reading of Job shows that it was the devil that had done all of the terrible things to Job, but Job didn't know it. The statement was an affirmation that he would trust God regardless of what happened to him.

A few years later, my sister and one of my older cousins became committed members in a small church in a neighboring city. In this church they believed in what they called "divine healing". They also spoke in other tongues. And even though I was mostly heathen, I knew enough about the Southern Baptist that they didn't speak in tongues. Well all of this made many in our family very uncomfortable.

One day, after getting off from working a summer job at the Community College where I worked as a Swimming Pool attendant and took lifeguard training, I decided to stop by my sister's house. She was preparing to go to her new church, but she neglected to invite me. I really didn't want to go, but I just wanted to be invited. So I stuck my foot in my mouth by commenting that she hadn't invited me and maybe she thought her new church was too good for me. She dropped her head and looked up at me with tears in her eyes saying: "Kenny there would be nothing in the world that would make me happier than for you to go to church with me tonight". Now I couldn't back out and I couldn't get my foot out of my mouth. I was trapped.

So I went to this little church. When I arrived I was very self-conscious. I had been in the pool all day so I was "ashy" and my "Afro" was

14

suffering as well from being wet. Black people understand what I'm talking about. I had on my Carson High Football shirt and gym trunks as well, so I just felt out of place. But as I sat through a traditional Vacation Bible School, nothing was said that really impressed me until near the end. Just before they dismissed for cookies and the worst punch you have ever tasted in your life, the Pastor had some closing remarks. During his remarks, he quoted John 10:10, which says: "The thief comes not but for to steal, kill and destroy. But I am come that you might have life and have it more abundantly".

The Pastor went on to explain that, in this verse, The Lord Jesus was doing the speaking. He went on to say that Satan or the devil was the one being referred to as the thief. Then the pastor said that Jesus was referring to Himself where it says, "I have come that you might have life and have it more abundantly". Finally the pastor said: "Anything that steals, anything that kills and anything that destroys life is from Satan and his demons. But anything that brings the abundant life comes from God and Jesus". He explained, among other things, that sickness and disease kill, steal and destroy life and therefore they were from the devil. But God had empowered Jesus to go about and do good and heal all that were sick and oppressed of the devil.

Acts 10:38 (AMP) "...God anointed *and* consecrated Jesus of Nazareth with the Holy Spirit and with power; and He went about doing good and, in particular, curing all who were harassed *and* oppressed by [the power of] the devil, for God was with Him.

To borrow an expression from Malcolm X, it didn't take my lightening fast mind long to realize that I had been hoodwinked, bamboozled...God didn't kill my mother; the devil did. And my hatred for God immediately left me. So I continued attending that Vacation Bible School for the remainder of the week. Then I just had one question for the lady who taught the teenagers. I said mam, if I get saved, will I have to stop partying.

You see, I was 17 and I loved to party. Though I was great in school (3.5 GPA), I lived for the weekends to go to some party somewhere. One thing I knew is that I wasn't going to quit and I wasn't going to be a hypocrite. So the lady responded: "Give your life to Jesus and if He wants you to stop partying He will tell you". Well I thought that was a good deal because I didn't think that God spoke to people; and even if He did, He would never speak to me.

So that Friday night, just before I got in the shower to get ready for whatever party I went to that night, I got down on my knees and invited Christ into my heart. Actually I did it in the bathroom with the door locked and the shower running for fear that someone might knock on my bedroom door and immediately walk in and catch me praying. (At this time I was living with one of my two brothers and he and his wife had a habit of doing the "quick knock and open the door" thing, without giving you a chance to react.)

When I invited Christ into my heart, no angels sang, no light filled my room or anything supernatural seemingly occurred. But what did happen is that it seemed as though a million pound burden lifted from my shoulders. It was similar to the experience that I had had in the third grade, and I knew in my heart that I was right with God. I went on to the party as usual and the rest of the night was uneventful.

However the difference between the first time and the second time was that I started going to church. Not for spiritual reasons either. There were a couple of sisters at that church that I was interested in. I had gotten "the digits" of one of them and started calling her for a couple of weeks. She asked me when I was coming back to church. So I started attending, thinking that I would stop when football season started, cause I had to watch my football games on Sunday.

Then one day, I came home from church and my brother confronted me about everything that was taking place in my life relative to all of this church business. He began to question me about other religions and philosophies, which he knew I was ignorant of. Wrong move. You see this was the devils way to try to confuse and discourage me and stop me from going to church. But it backfired. Actually, I decided after that conversation that no one would ever be able to ask me a question about what I believed without me being able to give them an answer from the Bible. I became consumed with the Bible. My godmother found out I was going to church and gave me a serious "study bible" by Finnis Dake. I spent hours in that

16

Bible the rest of that summer and I even decided not to play my senior year of high school football, to devote myself to my biblical studies.

As I studied the Bible and learned to pray, God would eventually reveal His plan for my life to me. I had intended on becoming a police officer, like my older brother, and work my way through college and become an attorney. (Even today when I preach and teach, I'm like an attorney pleading my case to the congregation.) While I was attending college, the Lord impressed me to read the Book of Jeremiah. Then He impressed me that just as He had called Jeremiah to be a prophet, before He formed him in his mother's womb, He had called me to preach and teach His Word.

Eventually I would begin preaching in that same small church and holding bible studies in homes and teaching in youth meetings. Finally, the Lord directed me to attend Rhema Bible College in Broken Arrow, Oklahoma. After graduation I served as the Youth Pastor and Senior Assistant Pastor at that church, Century Christian Center, for two and half years. Due to some of the things Pastor Robinson allowed me to implement and oversee, the church grew from an average attendance of about 65 (Adults and children) to over 250 (Adults and children) in about a year.

God would eventually call me to pastor. I pastored a church in Compton, CA for about 19 years, before the Lord led us to found the church here in Carson, CA. I trust that since you are reading this little book, you gave your heart to Christ here at Calvary Fellowship International.

I shared my story knowing that your story may be quite different from mine, but there may be some parts of my story that you can identify with. The point is that now that you are a follower of Christ, you have a story. Your story will consist of where you were when you came to Christ, how you came to Christ (the events that led directly to you receiving Him) and how you are now that you have received Jesus (obviously that part of your story is just beginning, but it will be just as awesome as the other parts one day). At Calvary Fellowship International, we encourage our members and our regular attenders who accepted Christ as their Lord and Savior to begin sharing their story from the start with their FFANS (Family, Friends, Associates,

Neighbors and even Strangers) to give them the same opportunity to become a follower of Jesus Christ that they received.

As you continue on with your spiritual growth, we at Calvary have embraced Rick Warren's Baseball Diamond Schematic to symbolize our discipleship process.

1st Base is our New Membership Orientation Class. It focuses on connecting people to Jesus Christ and our church.

2nd Base is our Spiritual Foundations Course, which focuses on the fundamental teachings of the Word of God that you need to grow spiritually.

3rd Base has two Courses. The first is the Ministry of Helps where we teach our members to recognize that serving is more than just volunteering, it is a ministry that God has called every believer to. The second course is called Spiritual Gifts. In it we teach you about the supernatural gifts that the Holy Spirit has made available to the body of Christ, so that we can serve Him at a supernatural level.

Home Plate is our Witnessing Institute. In all of these courses we encourage people to share their story, just as I have shared mine with you in this book, so that you can help others become followers of Jesus Christ. However in the Witnessing Institute, we give you specific teaching and training that will enable you to be more confident and therefore more effective in your sharing of Christ with the pre-Christians whom you know and will come in contact with.

If for some reason you are reading this book and you haven't yet invited Christ into your life, let me encourage you to pray the same prayer that I have led thousands into over these thirty-five years.

PLEASE PRAY THIS PRAYER AND MEAN IT FROM YOUR HEART...

Almighty God, I recognize that I am a sinner and I have no way of making up for my sins. But dear God thank you for providing your Son, the

18

Lord Jesus Christ, to die on the cross of CALVARY as the substitute for my sins. Lord Jesus, I believe that you are the Son of God. I believe that you died at CALVARY for me. I believe that God raised you from the dead. Sir, come into my heart, forgive me of all my sins and be the Lord and Savior of my life! By faith, I thank you for making God my heavenly Father and making me born-again and part of the family of God!

CHAPTER 1
REGISTER TO BE BAPTIZED IN WATER

Baptism separates the tire kickers from the car buyers. (Max Lucado)

[18] And Jesus came and spoke to them, saying, "All authority has been given to Me in heaven and on earth. [19] Go therefore and make disciples of all the nations, baptizing them in the name of the Father and of the Son and of the Holy Spirit, [20] teaching them to observe all things that I have commanded you; and lo, I am with you always, *even* to the end of the age." Amen. **Matthew 28:18-20 (NKJV)**

[15] And He said to them, "Go into all the world and preach the gospel to every creature. [16] He who believes and is baptized will be saved; but he who does not believe will be condemned. **Mark 16:15-16 (NKJV)**

Water baptism is something that is really found nowhere in our culture except in the church. So for many, it doesn't really make sense. However, this is something that Jesus command the early church to do with all of His new followers.

So the Bible is plainly telling us that once a person decides to follow Jesus as their Lord and Savior they MUST BE baptized in water. But there is much confusion about how one should be baptized in water. In some traditions, people are sprinkled with water and that is considered baptism. In other traditions people have water poured on them and that is considered being baptized in water.

Though this may be the tradition of some churches, this is not in keeping with the scriptures.

First of all the word from the Greek language that is translated as baptized is the word baptizo, meaning: to dip, to immerse, to submerge for a religious purpose (The Complete Word Study Dictionary).

Second, it is not in keeping with the example of our Lord Jesus Christ and those found in the book of Acts:

Matthew 3:13-17 (NLT) [13] Then Jesus went from Galilee to the Jordan River to be baptized by John. [14] But John tried to talk him out of it. "I am the one who needs to be baptized by you," he said, "so why are you coming to me?" [15] But Jesus said, "It should be done, for we must carry out all that God requires." So John agreed to baptize him. [16] After his baptism, as Jesus came up out of the water, the heavens were opened and he saw the Spirit of God descending like a dove and settling on him. [17] And a voice from heaven said, "This is my dearly loved Son, who brings me great joy."

Acts 8:36 (NLT) As they rode along, they came to some water, and the eunuch said, "Look! There's some water! Why can't I be baptized?"

Acts 8:38-39 (NLT) He ordered the carriage to stop, and they went down into the water, and Philip baptized him. [39] When they came up out of the water, the Spirit of the Lord snatched Philip away. The eunuch never saw him again but went on his way rejoicing.

As you see by these passages of Scripture, Jesus was fully immersed in water when He was baptized. Christ is our example in all things pertaining to faith. And it is not only important for you and me to be baptized (because in the passage above Jesus said that this is carrying our a requirement of God), but it is important for us to follow His example of being baptized. Then you see that the Ethiopian Eunuch was fully immersed in water as well. Neither Christ nor New Testament Christians were sprinkled with water or had water poured on their heads as the form or means of water baptism.

21

Well you may still be thinking, why does this really matter? The reason, of course, is what water baptism represents. Water baptism symbolizes two great biblical truths:

1.   The death, burial and resurrection of Christ!

        [3] I passed on to you what was most important and what had also been passed on to me. Christ died for our sins, just as the Scriptures said. [4] He was buried, and he was raised from the dead on the third day, just as the Scriptures said. **1 Corinthians 15:3-4 (NLT)**

2.   What has happened to you, now that you have received Christ as your personal Lord and Savior!

        [2] Of course not! Since we have died to sin, how can we continue to live in it? [3] Or have you forgotten that when we were joined with Christ Jesus in baptism, we joined him in his death? [4] For we died and were buried with Christ by baptism. And just as Christ was raised from the dead by the glorious power of the Father, now we also may live new lives. **Romans 6:2-4 (NLT)**

Remember this: Water Baptism is not what saves you. **Ephesians 2:8-9** tells us that we are saved by God's grace (or His unmerited favor) through faith. So there is no religious act that we can do to save ourselves;

including being baptized in water. We simply recognize that we are sinners in need of salvation, then we accept God's free gift of Salvation by making Jesus Christ our Lord.

Then, according **Romans 10:9,** the moment that we believe in our heart and say with our mouths that God raised Jesus from the dead and we take Him as our Lord, then we become saved. God then forgives and cleanses us from all of our past sins and we are instantly born again! So why then be baptized in water?

Water baptism is what we call at Calvary Fellowship International a Next Step. It is one of the first next steps that a believer should take after accepting Christ as your Lord and Savior. Also, water baptism is an expression of a public declaration that you are a Christ follower or one of Jesus' disciples!

Questions about Baptism

Q: When should I be baptized?

A: As soon as you have decided to receive Christ into your life, you can and should be baptized. There is no reason to delay.

Those who believe ... were baptized ... that day! —Acts 2:41

Then Philip began with the scripture and told him the Good News about Jesus. As they traveled along the road, they came to some water, and the man said, 'Look, here is water! Why shouldn't I be baptized right now?' Philip said, 'If you believe with all your heart, you may.' The man answered, 'I believe that Jesus Christ is the Son of God.' So they went down into the water and Philip baptized him. —Acts 8:35–38

Q: What if I was baptized as an infant? Must I be baptized again?

"Your infant baptism spoke of your parents' faith. Now, by being baptized as an adult, you honor your parents' faith because their hope when you were baptized as a baby was that you would follow Jesus. This new baptism allows you to decide to follow Jesus on your own."

23

Q: Can I be baptized together with my family and friends?

A: Yes! If each person fully understands the meaning of baptism, and each one has personally placed his or her trust in Christ for salvation, we encourage families to be baptized at the same time.

However, it is important to remember that baptism is a personal statement of faith, not a family or group tradition. It is usually not wise to delay your baptism while waiting on others to join you. This puts an undue pressure on them, and delays your obedience.

Q: What should I wear when I am baptized?

A: Women should wear shorts and a top or a swimsuit. Men should wear shorts and a T-shirt or a swimsuit. Bring a change of clothes, a towel, and a plastic bag for your wet clothes.

Q: What will happen at my baptism?

A: At the beginning of the service, one of the pastors will briefly explain the meaning of baptism. You will wait for your turn to be baptized. The pastor will introduce you, briefly lower you just under the water, and then raise you back up. Once you've been baptized, you can dry off and watch the others. Later you will receive your baptism certificate. We encourage you to invite your relatives and friends to attend your baptism.

CHAPTER 2
RESERVE TIME DAILY FOR PRAYER

"We never grow closer to God when we just live life. It takes deliberate pursuit and attentiveness." **Francis Chan**

Then He spoke a parable to them that men always ought to pray and not lose heart
Luke 18:1

Prayer is simply talking to God. But the Lord Jesus gave us what I call "a daily outline" for our devotional prayer life. (You will learn many other methods of prayer and important aspects of prayer as you grow spiritually, but this is the basis or foundation for an effective daily prayer life.)

Jesus gave His disciples a clear-cut plan or outline for prayer. It is commonly called the Lord's Prayer, but it should actually be called the disciples prayer. Jesus was a Jewish Rabbi or Master Teacher. In fact, He arrived at the highest level of being a teacher that Israel knew at that time. All Rabbis' gave their followers, students or disciples an outline for daily prayer and our Lord was no different

Some have thought and taught that this prayer is not valid for us today, because it doesn't mention praying in the name of Jesus. But my first pastor taught me years ago that any prayer that you pray begins by addressing the Father God, in the name of Jesus. Then it ends with thanking the Father God in the name of Jesus. What you place in between that is up to you, as long as it lines up with God's Word. He called it a prayer sandwich. The two pieces of bread were addressing and thanking the Father in the name of Jesus and ending the prayer in the name of Jesus. The meat is the body of the prayer.

The meat or the body of your prayer can be the outline that Jesus gave to His disciples. Again this is not a verbatim prayer that we are to quote, but a format, guideline or outline of prayer.

1. Our Father which is in Heaven, Hallowed be Your name...

This expression: "hallowed be your name" refers to God's name being magnified and treated with the utmost amount of respect. We are to pray that God's name be magnified, glorified and sanctified in this earth. Actually this occurs by what Jesus addressed in the next five points below. God is glorified when God's kingdom comes, His will is done, He gives us our daily bread, we forgive and are forgiven and when God helps us to overcome temptation. But before I go into these next five points, I want to point out something of great importance first. This first point in Jesus' prayer outline for us, His disciples, is that the primary motivation of our prayer is that God would magnify, glorify and sanctify His name as He brings to pass these next five things in the earth and in our lives!

There is a secondary inference here as it relates to "hallowed be Your name". It is a reminders that we should always start out our prayer with praise and worship of the Father God for all that He is and all that He has done for us! I read somewhere once, that there is only one thing that God can't do for Himself and that is to thank, praise and worship Himself!

Every morning you should thank and praise Him for watching over you and your family during the night. Thank Him for allowing and enabling you to awaken in your right mind, with the ability to use all of your physical and mental attributes. Thank Him for as many good things that exist in your life as you can. You may even consider writing out a list and bringing it with you into your place of prayer.

2. Thy Kingdom Come...

Jesus here tells us to pray about God's agenda. As you begin to read the gospels and other New Testament books of the Bible, you will begin to discover that Jesus came to establish the kingdom of God in the hearts of His followers. We, His followers, are supposed to extend or advance that Kingdom by doing several things: Preaching or telling people the good news that God wants them in His Kingdom and family; Telling them that they need to repent [or switch teams or kingdoms, from the kingdom of darkness onto the kingdom of God] (Matthew 4:7); Forcefully advancing God's kingdom by healing the sick, cleansing the lepers, raising the dead and casting out demons (Matthew 10:7-8; 11:11-12).

So, for my prayer time, I have strung together some of the verses that mention the kingdom of God and in my prayer time, I pray something like this each morning: "Heavenly Father, I pray that even he or she who is the least in your Kingdom will forcefully advance your kingdom today, by preaching that the kingdom of God is at hand, inviting people to turn their lives to you and by healing the sick, cleansing the lepers and aids victims, raising the dead and casting out demons somewhere in the earth today. I pray that the Kingdom of God that is within each and every believer (Luke 17:20-21) would somehow be revealed to us, in us and thru us today, in righteousness, peace and joy in the Holy Spirit (Romans 14:17) and for it to be manifested in power (1 Corinthians 4:20) in miracles, signs and wonders so that Christ's body, the church, may preach Your Word with all boldness (Acts 4:29-31).

3. Thy Will Be Done...

God's highest will on this earth is that not one person would go to hell. God wants every person to go to heaven. So we are to pray for those that we know, who aren't followers of Christ, to have the best person or persons possible to bring the gospel to them. We are to pray that God would open their eyes so that they can see and comprehend God's love for them. We are to pray that things occur in their lives that bring together these people so they can share the good news of God's love at the time when they are most open to receive it.

4. Give us this day our daily bread...

This is where we pray for our church, family and personal needs. Bread here doesn't just speak of literal bread, but everything necessary for us to live the abundant Christian life (Cp. John 10:10 Amplified Bible). One great teacher once said: "He who created the day created also its provision! Therefore while having sufficient food for today, it's the person of little faith that says: 'What shall I eat to-morrow?' So Jesus said: "Take no thought for your life, what ye shall eat or . . . drink. . . . . O ye of little faith. . . . Seek ye first the Kingdom of God, . . . and all these things shall be added to you".

These verses are not speaking against working, planning or saving; it's speaking against worrying when it doesn't look like we are going to make it. It's telling us to let God know that we trust that as we go about our business, doing what we know to do, that He will indeed make a way of provision for us. Then we can expect Him to add His supernatural strength, wisdom and power to our natural strength, wisdom and power. In **Deuteronomy 8:18 (NKJV)** God declared: [18] And you shall remember the LORD your God, for *it is* He who gives you power to get wealth, that He may establish His covenant which He swore to your fathers, as *it is* this day.

So we are to pray in faith, believing that God is going to give us the wisdom, the power and the strength to successful carryout our human efforts on our job or in our business, so that all of our needs are met, through Christ Jesus.

5. Forgive us this day as we forgive others...

You should incorporate daily praying for your family, friends, associates, neighbors and even strangers in this section. We call them FFANS here at Calvary. In several places in the New Testament, God says that our forgiving others is a requirement for Him forgiving us. Scriptures that address this include:

Matthew 6:12, 14-15 (NKJV)
[12] And forgive us our debts, As we forgive our debtors. [14] "For if you forgive men their trespasses, your heavenly Father will also forgive you. [15] But if you do not forgive men their trespasses, neither will your Father forgive your trespasses.

Mark 11:25, 26 (NKJV)
[25] "And whenever you stand praying, if you have anything against anyone, forgive him, that your Father in heaven may also forgive you your trespasses. [26] But if you do not forgive, neither will your Father in heaven forgive your trespasses."

Luke 6:37 (NKJV)
[37] "Judge not, and you shall not be judged. Condemn not, and you shall not be condemned. Forgive, and you will be forgiven.

Luke 17:3 (NKJV)
[3] Take heed to yourselves. If your brother sins against you, rebuke him; and if he repents, forgive him. [4] And if he sins against you seven times in a day, and seven times in a day returns to you, saying, 'I repent,' you shall forgive him."

The reason that Christ expects us to forgive others for what they have done to us is, because compared to what our sins did to Him (putting Him on the Cross), what others have done to us don't even compare. And listen to His words from the cross...

Luke 23:33-34 (NKJV) [33] And when they had come to the place called Calvary, there they crucified Him, and the criminals, one on the right hand and the other on the left. [34] Then Jesus said, "Father, forgive them, for they do not know what they do." And they divided His garments and cast lots.

Even as Christ hung from the cross, He extended forgiveness to those who crucified Him. That must be our attitude as Christians. We are to do this even before they ask us to forgive them and we are to do this daily so that their debts against us don't become so large that we are unwilling to forgive them.

6. Lead us not into temptation but deliver us from evil.

In the original Greek, which our New Testament manuscripts come from, the word evil has a definite article before it, making it deliver us from the evil or the evil one (Satan being the personification of evil).

In Matthew 13:19 and in 1 John 2:13, 14, the devil or Satan is referred to as the wicked or evil one. Actually, from a positional standpoint, we have been delivered from the kingdom or control of the devil according to Colossians 1:12-14.

Colossians 1:12-14 (NKJV) [12] giving thanks to the Father who has qualified us to be partakers of the inheritance of the saints in the light. [13] **He has delivered us from the power of darkness** and conveyed *us* into the kingdom of the Son of His love, [14] in whom we have redemption through His blood, the forgiveness of sins.

The word power in the above verse refers to the control or the authority of darkness. Darkness is a pseudonym for Satan's kingdom. We have been delivered from Satan's control; but not his temptations. The fact that our Lord says pray that we aren't led into

30

temptation let's us know that that is what is being referred to in regards to the evil one…not his control.

The book of James tells us this:

James 1:13 (NKJV) [13] Let no one say when he is tempted, "I am tempted by God"; for God cannot be tempted by evil, nor does He Himself tempt anyone. [14] But each one is tempted when he is drawn away by his own desires and enticed.

Therefore it is important that we pray that God would lead us around and guide us through Satan's various and daily attempts to get us off of our focus and off God's track into some area of distraction away from God.

CHAPTER 3
READ AND STUDY YOUR BIBLE

*"I believe the Bible is the best gift God has ever given to man. All the good
from The Savior of the world is communicated to us through this Book."*
                                                    — Abraham Lincoln

Study to show yourself approved of God, a workman that needs not to be
ashamed, rightly dividing the word of truth. 2 Timothy 2:15

Τhe second part of our devotional involves establishing a quiet spot
that you can go to and not be disturbed. It is also important that you
establish a specific time of the day that is best for you. If it is
possible, the mornings are usually the best because you want to always give
God your first and best. But some people are like me; night people. I am
more alert between 9:00 p.m. and 1:00 a.m. than any other time of the day.
Since I became married, began to pastor a church and raising children, I have
had to change my devotional time to the mornings. But if I were single, I
would still spend most of my devotional time at night. So whatever time of
the day you choose, just make sure that you are consistent with it.

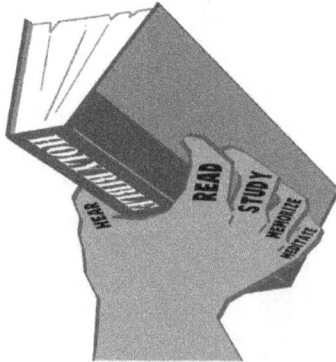

What should you do during this time of devotion? First, you should
begin a Bible reading plan of some sort. If you are a new Christian I would
encourage you to start reading the gospel of John. (I have included it in the
back of this book.) This is where I began my Bible reading in 1978. It is said

that the Gospel of John is God's love letter to the world. The greatest passage of Scripture ever penned can be found there! "For God so loved the world, that He gave His only begotten Son (Jesus), that whoever believes in Him would not perish, but have everlasting life" (John 3:16).

Once you have completed the gospel of John, you can expand your reading to include the other three gospels...Matthew, Mark and Luke. From there you may want to go on to read the entire New Testament. Or you could begin reading the book of Psalms from the Old Testament. This is one of the most inspirational books in the Bible. Then, finally you can go back to where it all started and read the Old Testament (from Genesis to Malachi).

And, no matter which plan you choose, I would encourage you to read one chapter from the book of Proverbs each day. There are 31 chapters. That basically gives you one per day and in months with only 30 days, you can read chapter 31 on those days. Another great help is by getting a "Devotional Book" such as The 365-Daily Devotional Commentary, or Trusting God Daily (by Joyce Meyers). This will help you with a powerful mini teaching from the Bible each day.

At the end of your reading time, be silent and wait to see what words, feelings, or images rise in your heart or tug at your thoughts. Notice what situations or people come to mind. Consider how the words or images connect with your life; then pray and ask the Holy Spirit to help you to see what God may be saying to you through what you have read, thought, and felt.

Say a prayer, asking God to help you follow the guidance you have received and to work on behalf of the people who came to mind during your reading and reflection. You may want to record your thoughts and feelings in a notebook or journal, to help you remember what God has been saying to you. Many people find it helpful to write about concerns and to write a prayer as a way to end their devotional time.

If you are just beginning to take time for reading the Bible and praying, plan to spend about ten minutes. As you become more comfortable with the process, you may find yourself spending a longer time.

OTHER IDEAS TO HELP YOU

• **Start small.** Use a resource such as *The Upper Room* that provides short, daily readings and guides you to look at small portions of scripture. Don't start off planning to spend 30 or 45 minutes for this is probably an unreasonable expectation that just may set you up for failure. You may want to start off with something manageable, like 10 or 15 minutes a day or even five or 10 minutes. The important thing is not the length of time, but the consistency that you develop.

• **Keep it manageable.** Don't set impossible goals such as reading an entire book of the Bible three times a day, every day. Choose a discipline that you can stick with.

• **Look for help.** If you are unfamiliar with the Bible, put a bookmark in the contents page of the Bible you use so you can turn there to find where each book begins. This will save time and help you avoid being frustrated when searching for a particular book of the bible. If you need help finding something to read that "speaks" to you, ask people at church for suggestions of what they have found helpful.

• **Find a spiritual "buddy."** Ask a friend, co-worker, or someone at our church to become your devotions partner. Then, each day, call or e-mail one another to discuss what you have read and what connections you make between the reading and your concerns.

• **Remember the value of having a pattern.** Finding a regular time and place to read the Bible and the day's meditation in *The Upper Room* helps most people be more consistent in turning their hearts to God. Regularity can become a rhythm that comforts, and having a familiar time and place may help you to settle into God's presence more easily.

• **Remember the value of being flexible.** Doing exactly the same things in the same way can become stale over time. If events in your day interfere with your usual pattern, find another time to read and reflect, or turn your mind to God by singing Christian song. Don't let a pattern control you and cause you discomfort. The point is to spend time with God, not to do this in a particular way.

- **Be creative.** Try something new from time to time. Here are some possibilities: Read your meditation outside. Write your prayers in a journal. Take a "prayer walk" with the intent of looking for God, and pray in response to the people and situations that come to mind as you walk. Listen to Christian music and talk to God about what it brings to mind.

The most important thing to remember, as we try to grow closer to God, is that God is already reaching out to us. God is the one who gives us the desire to grow, and God wants us to grow. We just keep showing up, even when we don't particularly feel holy or loving or eager. And we can trust that if we do so, God will show up, too.

CHAPTER 4
RECOGNIZE WHO YOU ARE IN CHRIST

For in him we live, and move, and have our being…**(Acts 17:20)**

When you made Jesus the Lord of your life, something happened to you. You were created in Christ Jesus. You were given an inheritance. Now, you are in Christ Jesus. You are born of God.

(Kenneth Copeland)

As you read through the New Testament, especially the epistles of Paul or the letters that he wrote to the churches, you will find several expressions, such as in Christ, by Christ, through Christ or in Him, by Him, and through Him. The casual uniformed reader of the Bible normally overlooks this, but these are some of the most important words in the New Testament. They have been called: "In Him Realities". To help you understand why, I want to share with you one of my favorite passages in the Bible:

Ephesians 2:4-10 (NKJV) [4] But God, who is rich in mercy, because of His great love with which He loved us, [5] even when we were dead in trespasses, made us alive together **with Christ** (by grace you have been saved), [6] and raised *us* up together, and made *us* sit together in the heavenly *places in Christ* Jesus, [7] that in the ages to come He might show the exceeding riches of His grace in *His* kindness toward us *in* Christ Jesus. [8] For by grace you have been saved through faith, and that not of yourselves; *it is* the gift of God, [9] not of works, lest anyone should boast. [10] For we are His workmanship, created *in Christ* Jesus for good works, which God prepared beforehand that we should walk in them.

This verse alone gives us four (really five – I combined two of them) In Him Realities…

1.   In the mind of God, when He raised Christ from the dead, we Christians were made alive spiritually **with** Christ;

2.   Then we were raised up together and made to sit together **IN** Christ!

3. So that God can show us the surpassing riches of His grace and kindness toward us **IN** Christ.

4. Because we are God's workmanship, created **IN** Christ Jesus to do good works that God has created us to carry out.

In this section I am sharing with you little known truths, which will make you a strong Christian, as you begin to discover these truths and claim them as your own. I pray that the revelation of the truth about who you are in Christ will rise up in your heart so that you can stand firm against the devil.

Some benefits of this position:

1. **Fellowship with God** – You now have the ability and the privilege to fellowship with God Almighty, the Creator of the Universe. When you accepted Christ, you didn't just get a religion with tons of rules to follow, but you received a relationship with God in which you became His very own child with the high privilege of fellowshipping with Him on a daily, hourly and even minute-by-minute basis. It begins with our daily devotion, as we discussed earlier, and it continues as we learn to practice the presence of God through out the day by obeying His written word, the Bible, and by talking with God and listening to that still small voice (See my C. D. Series called: "Beyond GPS – Discovering and Obeying God's Will For Your Life).

2. **Authority through Christ** – One of the things we as humans long for is a restoration of the original authority or dominion that was given to Adam and Eve in the Garden of Eden. This is not dominion or authority over people, but authority over the devil. The ability to govern your life and circumstances. God created Adam with this authority, but he forfeited it to the devil through sin. However, because of what Jesus did, this authority was hand delivered back to you and me.

3. **The ability to partake and enjoy everything God has provided for mankind through faith** – Jesus came and provided for us everything we need to live successfully on this earth. We appropriate these things by learning how to walk in Bible faith.

4. The ability to protect what God gave you to enjoy

There is a spiritual law that too few Christians are aware of and that is "The Law of Confession". This law, when properly understood, reveals to us that "Our Confessions Rule Us". Whenever people hear the word confession they instinctively think of confessing sin. And the Bible does say, "If we confess our sins, he is faithful and just to forgive us our sins, and to cleanse us from all unrighteousness" (I John 1:9). But that is only one side of the coin of confession; the negative side. But the Bible has much more to say about the positive side of confession than the negative side of confession. The positive side of confession is the confession of our faith in God the Father, in Jesus Christ, in the person and power of Holy Spirit and in God's Word.

Romans 10:9-10 (NKJV) says: [9] that if you confess with your mouth the Lord Jesus and believe in your heart that God has raised Him from the dead, you will be saved. [10] For with the heart one believes unto righteousness, and with the mouth confession is made unto salvation.

This does not refer to confessing sin. This is confessing Jesus as your Lord and Savior! In his heart man believes, and with his mouth h e confesses that Jesus is his Lord. By learning, believing and confessing or speaking out over your life what God's Word says about you, you develop and increase your faith concerning who you are in Christ. You will replace low self-esteem, low self-worth and insecurity with high Christ esteem and the security of who and what God has made you in Christ Jesus. I began doing that 35+ years ago, and today I can say that for over 30 years I have been free of what people think about me, so I can live, do and be as God desires me to live do and be!

A powerful principle of confessing what the Bible says about who we are in Christ is found in one of the most obscure books of the Bible; the book of Philemon. (Good things do come in small packages!)

38

Consider:

Philemon 1:4-6 (KJV): [4] I thank my God, making mention of thee always in my prayers, [5] Hearing of thy love and faith, which thou hast toward the Lord Jesus, and toward all saints; [6] That <u>the communication of thy faith</u> may become effectual <u>by the acknowledging of every good thing which is in you in Christ Jesus</u>.

By communicating your faith, through the power of confession, your faith will become more and more effectual or effective, as you acknowledge every good thing that is in you, in Christ Jesus! Begin saying who and what Christ is in you now and who and what you are in Christ.

For example:

Colossians 1:27 (NKJV): [27] ... "Christ in you, the hope of glory". Start saying that Christ (The Anointed King and His anointing) are in you and they are your hope of glory or heaven's glory.

2 Corinthians 5:21 (NKJV): [21] For He made Him who knew no sin *to be* sin for us, that we might become the righteousness of God in Him. Start declaring that you are not just an old sinner. But you are a sinner who has been saved by God's grace and you are now the righteousness of God in Him or in Christ!

According to **2 Corinthians 5:17**, you are a new creature (literally a new creation or species of being that never existed before) in Christ Jesus from the moment you became born again. You are a brand new person on the inside. If you are a new Christian, you will find a sort of dichotomy of desires in your life. Your body or flesh will still want to do all of the sinful things that it did before. But only now, you won't feel right about doing them before, during and especially afterwards. This is because your spirit, which is the real you has been cleansed from sin and made alive to God. You are a new person. And get this, in **2 Corinthians 5:21** the bible says, *that you were made the righteousness of God in Christ.* You are not righteous

39

in and of yourself, because according to **Isaiah 64:6**, our righteousness is as filthy rags. We traded our righteousness for His righteousness. We are righteous because of the shed blood of the Lord Jesus Christ. God sees you as he sees Christ, God sees you as brand new through the blood of Jesus.

Definitions of Righteousness:

1. The ability to stand in the presence of the Father without the sense of guilt and inferiority, as if sin never existed.

2. Right-standing with God.

3. Uprightness.

4. To be justified or declared right before God.

5. To be placed into a good position with God.

You must know and understand your position with God. It is not a license to sin and live anyway you want to. Rather, it is all the more reason to rely on the Lord to enable you to live a godly lifestyle. The quality of your understanding of your position with God, affects your ability to maximize the change that has occurred in your life. When you understand who you are, it will also affect the way you respond to problems, to people and to the promises from God's Word. The guilt and shame of your past is gone; covered in the blood of Jesus. You now have a good position with God because of who you are in Christ.

There is no room for low self-esteem or an inferiority complex because **you are** somebody in Jesus. You don't respond to life the same way that you used to.

As a student at Rhema Bible Training College, the late Dr. Kenneth E. Hagin, instructed me to "Find out what God's Word says about me and to make that my confession". He went on to say: "As a Christian, as a believer, read through the New Testament—primarily the Epistles. (The Epistles are the letters written to you the believer. They are written to the church.) As you read, look for all expressions such as, "in Christ," "in Him," "in Whom,"

40

"through   Whom," etc. With a colored pencil underline these expressions.

You will find approximately 140 such expressions, most of them in the Epistles. Some of these, however, don't exactly tell you something you have "in Christ." For instance, Paul's greeting in one Epistle is, "I greet you in the name of the Lord Jesus Christ." That has the expression "in Christ" but it doesn't tell you anything that is yours because you are "in Christ." You will also find other scriptures which convey the same message, but do not use the specific phrases, "in Him," etc. Yet they tell you who you are or what you are or what you have, because you are "in Christ." Now, when you find these scriptures—write them down. Then meditate on them.

Begin to confess them (or say them aloud out of your mouth). Begin to say with your mouth, "This is who I am, and this is what I am, and this is what I have, in Christ." For, you see, faith's confessions create life's realities. As far as God is concerned everything you have or are "in Christ" is (already) so. He has done it. Everything the Bible says is ours is ours legally. The Bible is a legal document, sealed by the blood of Jesus. However, it is your believing it and your confessing what it promises you that makes it a reality to you. God wants us to enjoy and know the reality of what He has provided for us—and His Word tells us how to do it!   (In Him - Kenneth E. Hagin).

At the end of this first part of the book, in Appendix 2, I have given an index of most, if not all, of the verses in the New Testament that mention these "In Him Realities". You should begin going over as many of them as possible as quickly as possible. However, it will take time for you to read, study, meditate upon and develop faith in them in order to begin to act like these verses are so. As you do this daily, you will see your spirit man develop and your faith grow and in 12 months, you will see how much you have grown spiritually.

CHAPTER 5
RECEIVE THE BAPTISM WITH
THE HOLY SPIRIT

But you shall receive power (ability, efficiency, and might) when the Holy Spirit has come upon you, and you shall be My witnesses in Jerusalem and all Judea and Samaria and to the ends (the very bounds) of the earth. **(Acts 1:8)**

Speaking with other tongues is not only the initial evidence of the Holy Spirit's indwelling; it is a continual experience for the rest of one's life. (Howard Carter - General Superintendent of the Assemblies of God of Great Britain)

What is The Baptism WITH The Holy Spirit?

The baptism in the Holy Spirit is an empowering for service that takes place in the life of the Christian

Two things happen when one receives the Baptism with the Holy Spirit:

First the believer is "filled" with the Holy Spirit to the point of overflowing! Every believer is born of the Spirit of God when they receive Christ, and thereby have a measure of the Holy Spirit in their heart and life. However when one receives the baptism with the Holy Spirit, as promised by our Lord in **Acts 1:8**, they receive the fullness of the Spirit and become endued or clothed with power!

The Lord revealed a distinction between these two experiences, when speaking about salvations when He told the woman at the well that when she received Him as the gifts of God it would be like receiving a well of water, spring up into eternal life.

42

John 4:10,14 (NKJV) [10] Jesus answered and said to her, "If you knew the gift of God, and who it is who says to you, 'Give Me a drink,' you would have asked Him, and He would have given you living water." [14] but whoever drinks of the water that I shall give him will never thirst. But the water that I shall give him will become in him a fountain of water springing up into everlasting life."

But in talking about receiving the baptism with the Holy Spirit, Jesus spoke of receiving the Holy Spirit as having rivers of living water flowing out of their heart.

John 7:37-39 (NKJV) [37] On the last day, that great *day* of the feast, Jesus stood and cried out, saying, "If anyone thirsts, let him come to Me and drink. [38] He who believes in Me, as the Scripture has said, out of his heart will flow rivers of living water." [39] But this He spoke concerning the Spirit, whom those believing in Him would receive; for the Holy Spirit was not yet *given,* because Jesus was not yet glorified.

To illustrate, if we drank water from a glass the water would be inside of us. In Salvation or the new birth, we not only get a glass of water, we get the whole well! In John 4, Jesus said that he would give the woman at the well living water, enough so that she would never be thirsty again. There he refers to salvation as a well of water. A well to blesses an individual and their family.

However, in **John 7**, at the Feast of Tabernacles, the Lord Jesus stood before the assembled masses to promise each of them not just a well of living water but living water comparable to a river. And not just one river, but multiple rivers flowing out them. The Jewish people there understood this to be an Old Testament reference found in the book of Ezekiel of living water that would bring healing to the nations!

So the difference between the two is that the first, the well, is to bring personal salvation and blessing to you. The second is so that God can use you to bring salvation and His miracle working power to the masses! Said another way, the Spirit of God in us as Christians reproduces the life of Jesus in us.

43

But this Baptism with the Holy Spirit, referring to those rivers of living water, reproduces the ministry of Jesus through us, including miracles and healings.

Why Do We Need The Baptism With The Holy Spirit?

Jesus said that when we receive this Spirit Baptism, that we would receive power beyond ourselves for service and ministry in His Kingdom.

When Jesus gave the Great Commission (**Matthew 28:19-20**), He knew that His disciples could not fulfill it in their own power. Therefore, He had a special gift in store for them: It was His plan to give them the same power that He had Himself -- the power of the Spirit of God. So, immediately after giving them the Great Commission, Jesus commanded his disciples not to leave Jerusalem, but to wait for what the Father promised, "which," He said, "you heard of from Me; for John baptized with water, but you shall be baptized with the Holy Spirit not many days from now" (**Acts 1:4-5**). He further promised: "You shall receive power when the Holy Spirit has come upon you; and you shall be My witnesses both in Jerusalem, and in all Judea and Samaria, and even to the remotest part of the earth" (**Acts 1:8**).

The disciples waited in Jerusalem as Jesus had commanded, and one day when they were all together, "suddenly there came from heaven a noise like a violent, rushing winds, and it filled the whole house where they were sitting. And there appeared to them tongues as of fire distributing themselves, and they rested on each one of them. And they were all filled with the Holy Spirit and began to speak with other tongues, as the Spirit was giving them utterance" (**Acts 2:3,4**).

Then Peter explained to the crowd that gathered that they were seeing the working of God's Spirit and told them about Jesus. The Christian church began that day with the disciples and three thousand people who joined them as a result of the day's events.

We can undertake making disciples of all nations with some degree of success without the baptism in the Holy Spirit, but when we do, we are undertaking a supernatural task with limited natural or human power.

It is God's will -- it is His commandment -- that we be baptized with, or filled with the Holy Spirit: "Be filled with the Spirit" (**Ephesians 5:18**). The knowledge and reality of the empowering Spirit enables us to reproduce the works of Jesus.

When May I Receive The Baptism In The Holy Spirit?

It can take place at the moment you confess faith in Christ, as in the case of the first Gentile convert and his family, Cornelius (**Acts 10:44-46**; **11:15, 16**); but often it occurs some time after the salvation experience (**Acts 8:12-17**).

Is There Anything To Fear?

Some people fear that if they ask for the baptism in the Holy Spirit, what they experience won't be the authentic working of the Spirit. But once they do ask for this experience, they are always glad they did. God doesn't cause us to do anything we don't want to, and all His gifts are good and perfect (**James 1:17**). Jesus said, "Now suppose one of you fathers is asked by his son for a fish; he will not give him a snake instead of a fish, will be? Or if he is asked for an egg, he will not give him a scorpion, will he? If you then, being evil, know how to give good gifts to your children, how much more shall your heavenly Father give the Holy Spirit to those who ask Him (**Luke 11:11-13**)?" The baptism in the Holy Spirit is an even better gift than any material gift you could receive, and God wants you to have it because He loves you and wants the very best for you.

How Do I Receive The Baptism In The Holy Spirit?

You only have to do three things:

First, once you have accepted Jesus Christ as your personal Lord and Savior, find a group of "Spirit-filled" believers to help guide you into the baptism with the Holy Spirit. This will be the easiest and quickest way. (If you are anywhere in Southern California, we would be glad to help you receive the fullness of God's Spirit. If not, just contact us and we will refer you to a Spirit-filled church so you can get the help that you need.

Second, when you connect to these believers, then all you have to do is ask God to baptize you with the Holy Spirit. The Bible says, "Ask, and it shall be given to you" (**Luke 11:9**).

Third, believe or "receive by faith" that you have in fact received this gift from God. The apostle Paul, writing to the Galatians, said, "Did you receive the Spirit by the works of the law, or by hearing with faith?" (**Galatians 3:2**). The answer, obviously, is faith. You have to believe that if you ask, you will receive.

Now, having asked and received begin to practice the power of the Spirit. An ideal place to begin is where the first apostles did, praising God in a new language. To do this, begin praising God out loud in whatever words come to you. Tell Him how much you love Him. Thank Him, worship Him, and yield your voice to Him. Now let Him give you new words of praise you never heard before. Praise Him with those words, too. You'll find that this will be a very rewarding experience of communicating with God that will build up your faith. Continue to pray to God each day in the language that the Holy Spirit has given you.

But this "prayer language" is just one of the gifts that God wants to give you through the baptism in His Spirit. The Word of God teaches that when we are filled with the Holy Spirit, we speak with other tongues as the Spirit of God gives utterance. It is the initial evidence or sign of the Holy

Spirit's indwelling us. **Acts 2:4** says, "*And they were all filled with the Holy Ghost, and began to speak with other tongues, as the Spirit gave them utterance.*"

What is the purpose for speaking in other tongues?

Six Reasons For Speaking In Other Tongues:

1) **Reason 1—Tongues assists believers in worshipping God**. The late Howard Carter said: Speaking in tongues is a flowing stream that never should dry up, for it will enrich a person's life spiritually. This agrees with Paul's saying that speaking in tongues will edify you.

2) **Reason 2—Tongues is edifies the believer spiritually.** In writing to the Corinthian church, the Apostle Paul stated in **1 Corinthians 14:4**, "*He that speaks in an unknown tongue edifies himself.*" So speaking or praying in tongues is a means of spiritual edification, or building up the believer spiritually.

    1 Corinthians 14:2 says, "*For he that speaks in an unknown tongue speaks not unto men, but unto God: for no man understands him; howbeit in the spirit he speaks mysteries.*" One translation of the New Testament says, "He speaks divine secrets."

    Paul is saying here that God has given the Church a supernatural means of communication with Himself. Notice that he said, "*My spirit prays.*" *The Amplified Bible* adds, "my spirit [by the Holy Spirit within me] prays." Jesus said, "God is a Spirit." You see, when you pray in tongues, your spirit prays. When you pray in tongues, your spirit is in direct contact with God, who is a Spirit, and you are talking to Him in a divine, supernatural language. Praise God!

3) **Reason 3—Tongues reminds the believer of the Holy Spirit's indwelling presence.**

    Speaking in tongues is a supernatural evidence of the Holy Spirit's indwelling. In Acts 10, the six Jewish Christians who journeyed with the

Apostle Peter to Cornelius' home were astonished because the gift of the Holy Spirit also was poured out on the Gentiles. They thought it was only for the Jewish church.

How did they know the Gentiles had received the gift of the Holy Spirit? **Acts 10:46** says, "*For they heard them speak with tongues, and magnify God.*" In other words, that was the supernatural or initial evidence of the Holy Spirit's indwelling.

Continued practice of speaking and praying in tongues helps us be conscious of the Spirit's presence. If I am conscious of the indwelling presence of the Holy Spirit every day, it is certain to affect the way I live.

I know from my own experience how easy it is, when one is not conscious of the Holy Spirit's presence, to lose one's temper or patience. But if you take time to fellowship with Him, speaking in tongues and praying, you can be conscious of His indwelling presence, and you will not do or say some of the things you do and say that cause you so much regret later.

4) **Reason 4—Praying in tongues is praying in line with God's perfect will.**

Praying in tongues eliminates selfishness from entering our prayers. If I pray out of my own thinking, my prayers may be unscriptural and selfish. Too often our prayers are like the old farmer's: "God my name is Jimmie and I'll talk all you'll give me."

Romans 8:26 says, "*For we know not what we should pray for as we ought.* " He did not say we did not know *how* to pray, because we do know how to pray. We pray to the Father in the Name of the Lord Jesus Christ. That is how to pray.

But just because I know how to pray, it doesn't mean I know exactly *what to pray for in every situation*. The verse in its entirety reads, "*Likewise the Spirit also helps our infirmities: for we know not what we should pray for as we ought: but the Spirit Himself makes intercession for us with groanings which cannot be uttered. "*

In looking into what the original language (Greek) that this verse was written in, we find that it says: "The Holy Spirit makes intercession for us with groanings which cannot be uttered in articulate speech" (articulate speech is the ordinary kind of speech). The Late Greek Scholar, Dr. P. C. Nelson pointed out that the Greek bears out that this inarticulate speech not only includes "groanings" in prayer, but also "other tongues."

That agrees with what Paul said in **1 Corinthians 14:14**, *"For if I pray in an unknown tongue, my spirit prays, but my understanding is unfruitful."*

People should be careful about making fun of speaking in tongues, because when a person prays in tongues, it is that person's spirit praying, aided by the Holy Spirit who is within him. So when you are mocking praying in tongues, you are actually mocking a work of the Holy Spirit.

I remember when I was a young child; I went to church with a friend where a lady was speaking in tongues. I came back home and mockingly told my mother what had taken place. I never saw her act the way she did. She reached out and grabbed me and told me to stop it. Then she said, "I was raised in a denomination where they don't speak in tongues…but it's in the Bible so I don't ever want to hear you doing that again! You are making fun of something that is a work of God.

5) **Reason 5—Praying in tongues stimulates faith.**

Speaking in tongues helps me to learn to trust God more fully. It helps my faith to speak in tongues. No, it will not *give* me faith; it *helps* stimulate my faith.

Jude 20 says, *"But ye, beloved, building up yourselves on your most holy faith, praying in the Holy Ghost.. .."* There is conclusive proof. Praying in tongues helps and stimulates my faith.

Because we don't understand with our minds the words, when we are speaking in other tongues, faith must be exercised to speak them. We have to trust God for it. And trusting God in one area will help us to trust God in another area. When one speaks in tongues, it helps them to believe God for other things because it stimulates faith.

6) Reason 6—Praying in tongues enables us to pray for the unknown.

Speaking in tongues provides a way for situations to be prayed for that no one knows about or thinks about. The Holy Spirit, on the other hand, knows everything. The Word of God says, "Likewise the Spirit also helps our infirmities: for <u>we know not what we should pray for as we ought</u>: but the Spirit itself makes intercession for us with groanings which cannot be uttered". **Romans 8:26**

My first experience along these lines occurred when I was just 18 years old. It was on a Friday evening that I had spent a great deal of time praying in other tongues. Near the end of that prayer time, I saw in a vision a woman whom I had never met. So obviously I wouldn't know that she needed prayer. I saw myself sharing scriptures on healing with her, and then laying hands upon her in prayer. Well the vision made no sense to me. I thought maybe the Holy Spirit was revealing how he wanted to use me in a healing ministry.

The next day, I shared with my sister what happened to me the night before. She told me that she, and a few people from church were going to pray for a lady with terminal cancer and invited me to go. So I went along with them. I was unprepared for what I would see. This lady had had her chest opened and then closed and was told to go home and wait to die. She looked like death warmed over. But this was the exact same lady that I saw in my vision. So I simply acted out what I saw in that vision, in terms of sharing the Bible and praying for her. The Lord's power went into her body and by the end of that week she was up on her feet, cancer free and driving around town; glory to God!

About two years later, while away in Oklahoma attending Bible College, one evening my sister had a heart attack. I was unaware of it.

No one was able to inform me, because I didn't have a phone. There was a two-hour difference between Los Angeles time and Tulsa time. So I had already gone to bed. But suddenly, I was awakened by the Lord and sat straight up in the bed. Somehow on the inside of me I knew that I needed to pray. Well I didn't know what to pray about, so I began praying in other tongues. After some extended time praying, I began to sense that someone was physically sick. So I continued praying. Again, after more time, I began to hear myself say Jan....Janice. Then I prayed more in tongues. Again, Jan...Janice...Janice.

My mind resisted, thinking that this couldn't be Janice, because she was fine and besides, she knew how to appropriate God's promises if she were attacked in her body. But I continued to pray for quite some time until I had, what Brother Kenneth E. Hagin referred to as, a note of victory in my spirit. Then I began praising God that everything was all right. I then went back to sleep.

Early the next morning, my landlord came knocking at my door. He informed me that he had received a call that my sister had had a heart attack and I needed to call home quickly. I did, but the only information that I got was the hospital my sister was in. She was in ICU, so I couldn't speak with her. But I was able to speak with her doctor. He told me that she had had a heart attack, but she was stable. Then when I found that out I asked the Lord to give my sister a new heart. I phoned the doctor again the next day and he informed me that she was doing much better. He said that they were running more tests. The next time I spoke with him, he said that the most recent test appears to show that she had a heart attack, but it was unclear. Then he said: "Just keep on praying reverend; your prayers are working". That's pretty good for a heart surgeon. The last time I spoke with him he told me that the first test showed that she had definitely had a heart attack; the last test shows that she never had a heart attack. It is my understanding that when a person has had a heart attack the EKG will continue to show that their heart was damaged at some point in time. But her doctor told me that every EKG that my sister has ever taken after the third one has never again shown that she ever had a heart attack. Praise God!

I could tell you story after story of experiences like this, glory to God! When all of this began, I had no means of communicating with the people back home. But, praise God for His supernatural communications system! Praying in other tongues is both scriptural and supernatural! All of us should pray in tongues, because then we can pray for things we don't even know that need to be prayed about. The baptism in the Holy Spirit, along with praying in other tongues are a supernatural gift that every believer can and should have to bless their lives and bless the lives of others!

CHAPTER 6
RECOGNIZE YOUR NEED TO
JOIN A GOOD LOCAL CHURCH

"…not forsaking the assembling of ourselves together, as *is* the manner of some, but exhorting *one another,* and so much the more as you see the Day approaching". **Hebrews 10:25 (NKJV)**

"Wherever we see the Word of God purely preached and heard, there a church of God exists, even if it swarms with many faults." (**John Calvin**)

The great 18th Century Evangelist, **John** Wesley, once said: "The Bible knows nothing of solitary religion." Christianity is based on fellowship (fellowship with God and fellowship with other believers). Following Christ means living in love, righteousness, and service and these things can be achieved only through the social relationships found in the church. Nothing can take the place of being a part of the local church.

As a new believer and follower of Jesus Christ, it is vital for you to get connected to a healthy, growing local church. You see, the best way for you to grow in your faith and learn more about this new life in Christ is through being around other believers who are also committed to learning and growing in Christ.

Participation in Christian fellowship through a local church body provides many benefits. You will grow in love, unity and spiritual maturity. You will be equipped, protected and encouraged so that you can become fruitful in God's kingdom. In short, you will become all that you can be only as you stay connected to a local corporate entity, known as the local church.

You were made to worship God! Worship is not just something that happens in a church service. Your daily life is an act of worship, as you live in a way that brings pleasure to God.

You are worthy, O Lord our God, to receive glory and honor and power. For you created all things, and they exist because you created what you pleased.

53

—Revelation 4:11

You bring pleasure to God when you:

* Love Him supremely

* Trust Him completely

* Obey Him wholeheartedly

* Praise Him continually

* Use your abilities

Every aspect of your life can be an expression of worship when you live in the realization and recognition of who God is and what He has done. Pastor Rick Warren writes in *The Purpose Driven Life:*

Every activity can be transformed into an act of worship when you do it for the praise, glory and pleasure of God.... How then is it possible to do everything for the glory of God? By doing everything as if you were doing it for Jesus and by carrying on a continual conversation with him while you do it.

Worship can happen anytime and anywhere. In fact, God calls us to a life of worship.

So here's what I want you to do, God helping you: Take your everyday, ordinary life—your sleeping, eating, going-to-work, and walking-around life—and place it before God as an offering. Embracing what God does for you is the best thing you can do for him.—Romans 12:1 (The Message)

Ways you can worship at Calvary Fellowship International:

* Attend a weekend service;

- Volunteer on Sunday morning or during the week;

- Give financially (The Tithe and an Offering)

When you became a Christian, you came into the family of God. In all healthy families, they get together at various times either through the day, the week, the month and certain holidays during the course of a year, to show their love, support, serve and care for one another. That's exactly what we do when we attend church. Sundays are the weekly times of fellowshipping together as we worship our loving and gracious Heavenly Father. It is also a time of instruction from our Father's word, the Bible.

Hebrews 10:24–25 (NLT) [24] Let us think of ways to motivate one another to acts of love and good works. [25] And let us not neglect our meeting together, as some people do, but encourage one another, especially now that the day of his return is drawing near.

The Christian life was not designed to be lived alone. The above verse is a direct command from God for believers not to neglect or forsake assembling together. The easiest and best way for you to assemble together with other believers is by going to church.

If you remain disconnected from membership of a local church, you are an orphan Christian, and you will grow up spiritually dysfunctional. Yes you may survive, but your Father God wants you to thrive! At Calvary our mission is to win the lost to Christ and to make bold, overcoming, victorious disciples (or followers) of Christ who multiply, dominate and make a difference in their own world and all over the world by giving them the best opportunity to become fully developing and fully engaged followers of Christ.

By connecting to a healthy and growing church like CFI, you will be able to grow strong as a Christian and become a blessing to others. You will learn to worship God through wonderful Christian music, learn the Word of God through great pastoral teaching, make new Christian friends that will encourage you in your walk and be able to use your talents to build and advance the Kingdom of God by becoming involved with a service team at Calvary.

Satan will try to convince you that you do not need to be concerned about other people. He will tell you that as long as you have God, you don't need other Christians. That's bologna! However, the truth is, we are one of the living stones that God is using to build a spiritual house (**1 Peter 2:5; Ephesians 2:20-22**). The house would be incomplete without you. You need other Christians, and they need you.

Actually, church membership and church attendance are not optional. In **Acts 2:41 (NKJV) the Bible tells us that:** "those who gladly received his word were baptized; and that day about three thousand souls <u>were added to them</u>". So from the very start, those who became followers of Christ became members of the local church.

Then in **Hebrews 10:24-25,** we are told: [24]And let us consider one another in order to stir up love and good works, [25]<u>not forsaking the assembling of ourselves together,</u> as *is* the manner of some, but exhorting *one another,* and <u>so much the more as you see the Day approaching.</u>

Not only should we become a member of a local church, we should attend as often as we can. Because Calvary's primary outreach focus is to previously unchurched people, many times they don't know what it means to attend church regularly. Well the Bible teaches that we should at least attend a worship service each Sunday. In fact, we should even be increasing our attendance much the more as we see the Day of Christ's second coming approaching.

[41] Then those who gladly received his word were baptized; and that day about three thousand souls were added *to them*. [42] And they continued steadfastly in the apostles' doctrine and fellowship, in the breaking of bread, and in prayers. **Acts 2:41-42 (NKJV)**

Spiritually, this is where connecting with a local church and becoming a member is important. In this passage of the Acts of Apostles, this was the beginning of the church...the very first day! Peter preached to thousands on that very first day. Three thousand people accepted Christ as their Lord and Savior that day! And these people did four things:

First, they continued steadfastly (or consistently) in the apostles doctrine or teaching.

The other thing is this: Now that you have received Christ, the Bible calls you spiritually a newly born "babe" in Christ. So just like any new babe, you need to be connected to a family if you are going to survive, grow and thrive. Responsible parents do not abandon their children. They make sure to care and provide for them. God is your heavenly Father, and He cares for you and each person who comes to Him through faith in the Lord Jesus Christ. There is no such thing as a healthy, lone-ranger Christian. Even the Lone Ranger had Tanto!

Our Heavenly Father shows His love for us by putting us into the safety of a loving and caring family of believers like CFI that will help you to grow to spiritual maturity. Within CFI, you can receive pastoral oversight from the senior pastor, ministerial staff and other leaders. "Their work is to watch over your souls, and they know they are accountable to God" **(Hebrews 13:17 NLT)**.

In addition to receiving pastoral instruction in our worship services, our goal is to get you involved in Sunday School or one of the Small Groups that meet weekly in a home. In these ministries you will receive the individual care and attention that you need to grow into an effective disciple of Christ.

Second, they continued consistently in fellowshipping with one another.

The New Testament was originally written in Greek. The word that is translated "fellowship" is the Greek word koinonia, and means "communion", or "sharing in common" (see **Acts 2:42; 1 John 1:7**). This word describes how Christians should live; that is as a community of people who share the selfless, sacrificial agape (God kind of love).

The Bible tells us that the early church believed strongly in fellowship. It says that: "Day by day continuing with one mind in the temple, and breaking bread from house to house, they were taking their meals together with gladness and sincerity of heart" **(Acts 2:46 NASB).**

The English poet John Donne said, "No man is an island", and that is particularly true in the body of Christ. When you are born again, you become part of a spiritual family that is just as real as your natural family. To isolate yourself from your Christian brothers and sisters is to isolate yourself from the expression of Christ on the earth. In my 30 plus years as a Christian, I have found that God speaks to me just as much through other believers as He does directly through the Holy Spirit...when I'm sensitive to God.

The Lord Jesus gave the church a commandment that we must follow:

"This is My commandment, that you love one another, just as I have loved you. "Greater love has no one than this that one lay down his life for his friends. "You are My friends if you do what I command you. "No longer do I call you slaves, for the slave does not know what his master is doing;

but I have called you friends, for all things that I have heard from My Father I have made known to you" **(John 15:12-15 NASB).**

This is how we know what love is: Jesus Christ laid down His life for us. And we ought to lay down our lives for our brothers...Dear children, let us not love with words or tongue but with actions and in truth" **(1 Johns 3:16, 18).**

This commandment cannot be followed with out you and I being connected to a local church. Notice it says: Love one another. This is talking about loving each other as Christians. We all have a love for our natural family members, but Jesus here commands us to love our spiritual family members. Without being a part of a local church, which becomes your spiritual family, you cannot obey this commandment.

Third, they continued to partake of the Lord's Supper or Holy Communion (i.e., the breaking of bread).

Finally, they continued steadfastly in prayer.

Then notice what the rest of that passage in Acts 2 says:

[46] The believers shared a common purpose, and every day they spent much of their time together in the Temple (public worship services) area. They also ate together in their homes (small group services). They were happy to share their food and ate with joyful hearts. [47] The believers praised God and were respected by all the people. More and more people were being saved every day, and the Lord was adding them to their group. **Acts 2:46-47.**

Not only do you need to attend church for corporate Bible study, fellowship, Holy Communion and Prayer, but you need to become a member of a local church to connect to the common purpose of that church; which we called vision. Take a look at these verses:

Proverbs 29:18 says: Where there is no vision, the people perish: but he that keeps the law (God's Word), happy is he.

Proverbs 29:18 (AMP): Where there is no vision [no redemptive revelation of God], the people perish; but he who keeps the law [of God, which includes that of man]—blessed (happy, fortunate, and enviable) is he.

Proverbs 29:18 (NLT): When people do not accept divine guidance, they run wild. But whoever obeys the law is joyful.

Proverbs 29:18 (MSG): If people can't see what God is doing, they stumble all over themselves; But when they attend to what he reveals, they are most blessed.

You need to join a local church so you can have a pastor that will share God's vision or God's redemptive revelation with you, so that you won't just be running wild or stumbling all over yourself spiritually speaking. Then, together with your local church, you can attend to what God reveals and be most blessed!

The Bible tells us that God has a wonderful plan for your life...

Jeremiah 29:10-11 (NLT): [10]This is what the LORD says: [11] For I know the plans I have for you," says the LORD. "They are plans for good and not for disaster, to give you a future and a hope.

The Bible also tells us that He has created you to do some great things...

Ephesians 2:8-10 (AMP): [8]For it is by free grace (God's unmerited favor) that you are saved (delivered from judgment *and* made partakers of Christ's salvation) through [your] faith. And this [salvation] is not of yourselves [of your own doing, it came not through your own striving], but it is the gift of God; [9]Not because of works [not the fulfillment of the Law's demands], lest any man should boast. [It is not the result of what anyone can possibly do, so no one can pride himself in it or take glory to himself.] [10]For we are God's own handiwork (His workmanship), recreated in Christ Jesus, [born anew] that we may do those good works which God predestined (planned beforehand) for us [taking paths which He prepared ahead of time], that we should walk in them [living the good life which He prearranged and made ready for us to live].

60

When you get connected with a local church you will see God's plan for your life begin to unfold. God has given each and every one of us our own unique gifts and talents...

Romans 12:4-8 (NKJV): ⁴For as we have many members in one body, but all the members do not have the same function, ⁵so we, *being* many, are one body in Christ, and individually members of one another. ⁶Having then gifts differing according to the grace that is given to us, *let us use them;* if prophecy, *let us prophesy* in proportion to our faith; ⁷or ministry, *let us use it* in *our* ministering; he who teaches, in teaching; ⁸he who exhorts, in exhortation; he who gives, with liberality; he who leads, with diligence; he who shows mercy, with cheerfulness.

God wants us to combine our gifts and talents with others in a local church body in order to encourage, serve, teach, lead and bless one another with cheerfulness and mercy and to reach the World with the message of the good news of salvation!

You should become a committed and dedicated member of a local church where there is a real sense of purpose or vision. You should find a church where the people are happy and joyful as they share their lives together with one another. You should find a church where there is joyous praise and worship of God taking place and where there is no hint of sexual or financial scandal among its leadership. This will be a church that is respected by all the people.

Finally, this church should be a church that is aggressively reaching out to the unsaved in their neighborhood, community and city. And you should get behind that vision and start actively reaching out to your FFANS (or Family, Friends, Associates, Neighbors and even Strangers), talking to them about what God has done in your life and inviting and bringing them to church; especially on what our church calls "Big Days". Large or small, old or young, this is the kind of church where the blessing of the Lord will abide!

Your Story

Take a few minutes to write out your story of becoming a Christian. This is the beginning of your testimony and will be a powerful tool as you start to share Christ with others in your life:

A Final Thought

You are a new creation on a new journey. I hope that you will take these six Next Steps we've discussed to heart. Take the time to write out your story; thinking about what God has brought you through. And spend some time studying the statement of beliefs and all of the verses that substantiate those beliefs (in Appendix 4) because they will help you to gain greater understanding of your newfound faith. Now that you have become a Christian you should do all you can to seek, study, and learn about the life that is now yours through Christ.

I trust that this book has been and will continue to be helpful to you as you start walking your new path. It isn't meant to answer every single one of your questions. No book could ever do that. The truth is that I can't tell you every twist and turn that your journey with God is going to take, because I don't know. That's the beauty of a relationship; you jump in and see where it leads. Enjoy the journey.

No eye has seen, no ear has heard, and no mind has imagined what God has prepared for those who love him.

—1 Corinthians 2:9–10

Appendix 1
How Can I Be Sure of God's Forgiveness?

Sometimes, after accepting Jesus into our lives, we begin to doubt whether His forgiveness really covers all of our past mistakes. We wonder if Jesus dying on the cross was enough to truly cover every one of our sins. What we are actually questioning is the assurance of our salvation. These doubts may surface because of a persistent sin, a personal crisis, or a feeling of separation from God.

God wants us to have the full assurance that He loves us and that, because we have asked Jesus to be our Lord, He has forgiven us – completely. The doubts and uncertainties that creep up are not from God. When we face such questions, we must rely on his promises rather than on our own judgment or emotions. In on our own understanding, we are likely to minimize the significance of what God has done.

Don't worry about anything; instead, pray about every- thing. Tell God what you need, and thank him for all he has done. Then you will experience God's peace, which exceeds anything we can understand. His peace will guard your hearts and minds as you live in Christ Jesus.

Philippians 4:6-7

To overcome doubts, spend some time meditating on the single most important fact about salvation. Here it is: Salvation is a gift from God.

God saved you by his grace when you believed. And you can't take credit for this; it is a gift from God. Salvation is not a reward for the good things we have done, so none of us can boast about it.

- Ephesians 2:8,9

God is so serious about saving us from our sins that he sent Jesus into this world as a sacrifice. God freely forgives us, and gives us purpose, when we confess our sin to him and ask his son to come into our lives as our leader and director.

"For God loved the world so much that he gave his one and only Son, so that everyone who believes in him will not perish but have eternal life. God sent his Son into the world not to judge the world, but to save the world through him."

- John 3:16,17

When a new Christian questions whether or not he has experienced true forgiveness, he needs to look back to his original decision to begin a relationship with Jesus. If he was serious about becoming a follower of Jesus and receiving forgiveness for his past mistakes, then God is just as serious about engaging in that relationship.

My sheep listen to my voice; I know them, and they follow me. I give them eternal life, and they will never perish. No one can snatch them away from me, for my Father has given them to me, and he is more powerful than anyone else. No one can snatch them from the Father's hand."

- John 10:27-29.

We can rest in the assurance of our salvation with- out doubt because salvation does not depend on us – it depends on God. And he is trustworthy.

Several issues common to our human nature could lead you to doubt whether or not you are truly a follower of Jesus. Here are some struggles that you may experience:

☐ **Placing too much emphasis on emotions** Becoming a follower of Jesus is usually expressed in terms of feelings, but the assurance of our salvation is found in the significance of God's gift to us. We do not become followers of Jesus based on a feeling, but rather based on the start of a relationship with Jesus. We can trust him even when our own faith is weak, when we have done wrong, or when he feels distant. Think about this promise from scripture:

Our actions will show that we belong to the truth, so we will be confident when we stand before God.

Even if we feel guilty, God is greater than our feelings, and he knows

65

everything.

- 1 John 3:19,20

Comparing your experience with someone else's experience. Sometimes, when we hear other people's stories about how they came to accept Jesus, we begin to question our own salvation experience. If our story is different, or if someone else seems closer to God than we feel, we may start to wonder, "Am I really a Christian?" or "Why don't I have that kind of relationship with God?"

We are all uniquely crafted. God made us with different personalities and different ways of relating. You are an individual. You will never relate to God exactly like someone else – someone who has a different temperament and background of experiences – and you shouldn't want to. Thankfully, we can affirm and celebrate the dynamic ways God reveals himself to other people without allowing them to be negative reflections on our own experience and relationship with our Father.

Doubting God's love after a period of falling away. Understand that being a follower of Jesus does not mean that you will never again be tempted, or that you'll never make another mistake. We are all still human and we have to work at growing into fully-developing followers of Christ. Even when you stumble, God still loves you because you are his child. 1 John 1:8-9 tells us how to deal with our times of failure:

If we claim we have no sin, we are only fooling ourselves and not living in the truth. But if we confess our sins to him, he is faithful and just to forgive us our sins and to cleanse us from all wickedness (1 John 1:8,9).

Remember what we said earlier – becoming a follower of Jesus is both an event and a process.

If we have committed ourselves to God as he has made himself known to us, we have his assurance of our eternal security. We cannot lose the salvation that he has sealed with the sacrifice of his son. If we have sincerely asked for forgiveness for our sins and invited Jesus into our lives, we can trust that we are new, forgiven creatures in right relationship with God.

Yes, turn to our God, for he will forgive generously (Isaiah 55:7).

APPENDIX 2
(Who You Are In and Through Christ)

IN CHRIST

Romans 3:24 All are justified and made upright and in right standing with God, freely and gratuitously by His grace (His unmerited favor and mercy), through the redemption, which is [provided] in Christ Jesus.

Romans 6:11 Even so consider yourselves also dead to sin and your relation to it broken, but alive to God [living in unbroken fellowship with Him] in Christ Jesus.

Romans 8:1 Therefore, [there is] now no condemnation (no adjudging guilty of wrong) for those who are in Christ Jesus, who live [and] walk not after the dictates of the flesh, but after the dictates of the Spirit.

Romans 8:2 For the law of the Spirit of life [which is] in Christ Jesus [the law of our new being] has freed me from the law of sin and of death.

Romans 12:5 So we, numerous as we are, are one body in Christ (the Messiah) and individually we are parts one of another [mutually dependent on one another].

1 Corinthians 1:2 To the church (assembly) of God which is in Corinth, to those consecrated and purified and made holy in Christ Jesus, [who are] selected and called to be saints (God's people), together with all those who in any place call upon and give honor to the name of our Lord Jesus Christ, both their Lord and ours.

1 Corinthians 1:4 I thank my God at all times for you because of the grace (the favor and spiritual blessing) of God which was bestowed on you in Christ Jesus.

1 Corinthians 1:30 But it is from Him that you have your life in Christ Jesus, Whom God made our Wisdom from God, [revealed to us a knowledge of the divine plan of salvation previously hidden, manifesting itself as] our Righteousness [thus making us upright and putting us in right standing with God], and our Consecration [making us pure and holy], and our Redemption [providing our ransom from eternal penalty for sin].

1 Corinthians 15:22 For just as [because of their union of nature] in Adam all people die, so also [by virtue of their union of nature] shall all in Christ be made alive.

2 Corinthians 1:21 But it is God Who confirms and makes us steadfast and establishes us [in joint fellowship] with you in Christ, and has consecrated and anointed us [enduing us with the gifts of the Holy Spirit].

2 Corinthians 2:14 But thanks be to God, Who in Christ always leads us in triumph [as trophies of

Christ's victory] and through us spreads and makes evident the fragrance of the knowledge of God everywhere.

2 Corinthians 3:14 In fact, their minds were grown hard and calloused [they had become dull and had lost the power of understanding]; for until this present day, when the Old Testament (the old covenant) is being read, that same veil still lies [on their hearts], not being lifted [to reveal] that in Christ it is made void and done away.

2 Corinthians 5:17 Therefore if any person is [engrafted] in Christ (the Messiah) he is a new creation (a new creature altogether); the old [previous moral and spiritual condition] has passed away. Behold, the fresh and new has come!

2 Corinthians 5:19 It was God [personally present] in Christ, reconciling and restoring the world to favor with Himself, not counting up and holding against [men] their trespasses [but cancelling them], and committing to us the message of reconciliation (of the restoration to favor).

Galatians 2:4 [My precaution was] because of false brethren who had been secretly smuggled in [to the Christian brotherhood]; they had slipped in to spy on our liberty and the freedom which we have in Christ Jesus, that they might again bring us into bondage [under the Law of Moses].

Galatians 2:16 Yet we know that a man is justified or reckoned righteous and in right standing with God not by works of the Law, but [only] through faith and [absolute] reliance on and adherence to and trust in Jesus Christ (the Messiah, the Anointed One). [Therefore] even we [ourselves] have believed on Christ Jesus, in order to be justified by faith in Christ and not by works of the Law [for we cannot be justified by any observance of the ritual of the Law given by Moses], because by keeping legal rituals and by works no human being can ever be justified (declared righteous and put in right standing with God).

Galatians 3:26 For in Christ Jesus you are all sons of God through faith.

Galatians 3:28 There is [now no distinction] neither Jew nor Greek, there is neither slave nor free, there is not male and female; for you are all one in Christ Jesus.

Galatians 5:6 For [if we are] in Christ Jesus, neither circumcision nor uncircumcision counts for anything, but only faith activated and energized and expressed and working through love.

Galatians 6:15 For neither is circumcision [now] of any importance, nor uncircumcision, but [only] a new creation [the result of a new birth and a new nature in Christ Jesus, the Messiah].

Ephesians 1:3 May blessing (praise, laudation, and eulogy) be to the God and Father of our Lord Jesus Christ (the Messiah) Who has blessed us in Christ with every spiritual (given by the Holy Spirit) blessing in the heavenly realm!

Ephesians 1:4 Even as [in His love] He chose us [actually picked us out for Himself as His own] in

Christ before the foundation of the world, that we should be holy (consecrated and set apart for Him) and blameless in His sight, even above reproach, before Him in love.

Ephesians 1:10 [He planned] for the maturity of the times and the climax of the ages to unify all things and head them up and consummate them in Christ, [both] things in heaven and things on the earth.

Ephesians 1:12 So that we who first hoped in Christ [who first put our confidence in Him have been destined and appointed to] live for the praise of His glory!

Ephesians 2:6 And He raised us up together with Him and made us sit down together [giving us joint seating with Him] in the heavenly sphere [by virtue of our being] in Christ Jesus (the Messiah, the Anointed One).

Ephesians 2:7 He did this that He might clearly demonstrate through the ages to come the immeasurable (limitless, surpassing) riches of His free grace (His unmerited favor) in [His] kindness and goodness of heart toward us in Christ Jesus.

Ephesians 2:10 For we are God's [own] handiwork (His workmanship), recreated in Christ Jesus, [born anew] that we may do those good works which God predestined (planned beforehand) for us [taking paths which He prepared ahead of time], that we should walk in them [living the good life which He prearranged and made ready for us to live].

Ephesians 2:13 But now in Christ Jesus, you who once were [so] far away, through (by, in) the blood of Christ have been brought near.

Ephesians 3:6 [It is this:] that the Gentiles are now to be fellow heirs [with the Jews], members of the same body and joint partakers [sharing] in the same divine promise in Christ through [their acceptance of] the glad tidings (the Gospel).

Philippians 3:14 I press on toward the goal to win the [supreme and heavenly] prize to which God in Christ Jesus is calling us upward.

Philippians 4:7 And God's peace [shall be yours, that tranquil state of a soul assured of its salvation through Christ, and so fearing nothing from God and being content with its earthly lot of whatever sort that is, that peace] which transcends all understanding shall garrison and mount guard over your hearts and minds in Christ Jesus.

Philippians 4:13 I have strength for all things in Christ Who empowers me [I am ready for anything and equal to anything through Him Who infuses inner strength into me; I am self-sufficient in Christ's sufficiency].

Philippians 4:19 And my God will liberally supply (fill to the full) your every need according to His riches in glory in Christ Jesus.

Colossians 1:28 Him we preach and proclaim, warning and admonishing everyone and instructing everyone in all wisdom comprehensive insight into the ways and purposes of God), that we may present every person mature (full-grown, fully initiated, complete, and perfect) in Christ (the Anointed One).

1 Thessalonians 4:16 For the Lord Himself will descend from heaven with a loud cry of summons, with the shout of an archangel, and with the blast of the trumpet of God. And those who have departed this life in Christ will rise first.

1 Thessalonians 5:18 Thank [God] in everything [no matter what the circumstances may be, be thankful and give thanks], for this is the will of God for you [who are] in Christ Jesus [the Revealer and Mediator of that will].

1 Timothy 1:14 And the grace (unmerited favor and blessing) of our Lord [actually] flowed out superabundantly and beyond measure for me, accompanied by faith and love that are [to be realized] in Christ Jesus.

2 Timothy 1:1 Paul, an apostle (special messenger) of Christ Jesus by the will of God, according to the promise of life that is in Christ Jesus.

2 Timothy 1:9 [For it is He] Who delivered and saved us and called us with a calling in itself holy and leading to holiness [to a life of consecration, a vocation of holiness]; [He did it] not because of anything of merit that we have done, but because of and to further His own purpose and grace (unmerited favor) which was given us in Christ Jesus before the world began [eternal ages ago].

2 Timothy 1:13 Hold fast and follow the pattern of wholesome and sound teaching which you have heard from me, in [all] the faith and love which are [for us] in Christ Jesus.

2 Timothy 2:1 So you, my son, be strong (strengthened inwardly) in the grace (spiritual blessing) that is [to be found only] in Christ Jesus.

2 Timothy 2:10 Therefore I [am ready to] persevere and stand my ground with patience and endure everything for the sake of the elect [God's chosen], so that they too may obtain [the] salvation which is in Christ Jesus, with [the reward of] eternal glory.

2 Timothy 3:15 And how from your childhood you have had a knowledge of and been acquainted with the sacred Writings, which are able to instruct you and give you the understanding for salvation which comes through faith in Christ Jesus [through the leaning of the entire human personality on God in Christ Jesus in absolute trust and confidence in His power, wisdom, and goodness].

Philemon 1:6 [And I pray] that the participation in and sharing of your faith may produce and promote full recognition and appreciation and understanding and precise knowledge of every good [thing] that is ours in [our identification with] Christ Jesus [and unto His glory].

1 Peter 5:10 And after you have suffered a little while, the God of all grace [Who imparts all blessing and favor], Who has called you to His [own] eternal glory in Christ Jesus, will Himself complete and make you what you ought to be, establish and ground you securely, and strengthen, and settle you.

IN HIM

John 1:4 In Him was Life, and the Life was the Light of men.

John 3:15 In order that everyone who believes in Him [who cleaves to Him, trusts Him, and relies on Him] may not perish, but have eternal life and [actually] live forever!

John 3:16 For God so greatly loved and dearly prized the world that He [even] gave up His only begotten (unique) Son, so that whoever believes in (trusts in, clings to, relies on) Him shall not perish (come to destruction, be lost) but have eternal (everlasting) life.

Acts 17:28 For in Him we live and move and have our being; as even some of your [own] poets have said, for we are also His offspring.

1 Corinthians 1:5 [So] that in Him in every respect you were enriched, in full power and readiness of speech [to speak of your faith] and complete knowledge and illumination [to give you full insight into its meaning].

2 Corinthians 1:20 For as many as are the promises of God, they all find their Yes [answer] in Him [Christ]. For this reason we also utter the Amen (so be it) to God through Him [in His Person and by His agency] to the glory of God.

2 Corinthians 5:21 For our sake He made Christ [virtually] to be sin Who knew no sin, so that in and through Him we might become endued with, viewed as being in, and examples of] the righteousness of God [what we ought to be, approved and acceptable and in right relationship with Him, by His goodness].

Ephesians 1:7 In Him we have redemption (deliverance and salvation) through His blood, the remission (forgiveness) of our offenses (shortcomings and trespasses), in accordance with the riches and the generosity of His gracious favor.

Ephesians 1:11 In Him we also were made [God's] heritage (portion) and we obtained an inheritance; for we had been foreordained (chosen and appointed beforehand) in accordance with His purpose, Who works out everything in agreement with the counsel and design of His [own] will.

Ephesians 1:13 In Him you also who have heard the Word of Truth, the glad tidings (Gospel) of your salvation, and have believed in and adhered to and relied on Him, were stamped with the seal of the long-promised Holy Spirit.

Ephesians 2:21 In Him the whole structure is joined (bound, welded) together harmoniously, and it continues to rise (grow, increase) into a holy temple in the Lord [a sanctuary dedicated, consecrated, and sacred to the presence of the Lord].

Ephesians 2:22 In Him [and in fellowship with one another] you yourselves also are being built up [into this structure] with the rest, to form a fixed abode (dwelling place) of God in (by, through) the Spirit.

Philippians 3:9 And that I may [actually] be found and known as in Him, not having any [self-achieved] righteousness that can be called my own, based on my obedience to the Law's demands (ritualistic uprightness and supposed right standing with God thus acquired), but possessing that [genuine righteousness] which comes through faith in Christ (the Anointed One), the [truly] right standing with God, which comes from God by [saving] faith.

Colossians 1:16 For it was in Him that all things were created, in heaven and on earth, things seen and things unseen, whether thrones, dominions, rulers, or authorities; all things were created and exist through Him [by His service, intervention] and in and for Him.

Colossians 1:17 And He Himself existed before all things, and in Him all things consist (cohere, are held together).

Colossians 2:3 In Him all the treasures of [divine] wisdom (comprehensive insight into the ways and purposes of God) and [all the riches of spiritual] knowledge and enlightenment are stored up and lie hidden.

Colossians 2:7 Have the roots [of your being] firmly and deeply planted [in Him, fixed and founded in Him], being continually built up in Him, becoming increasingly more confirmed and established in the faith, just as you were taught, and abounding and overflowing in it with thanksgiving.

Colossians 2:10 And you are in Him, made full and having come to fullness of life [in Christ you too are filled with the Godhead--Father, Son and Holy Spirit--and reach full spiritual stature]. And He is the Head of all rule and authority [of every angelic principality and power].

Colossians 2:11 In Him also you were circumcised with a circumcision not made with hands, but in a [spiritual] circumcision [performed by] Christ by stripping off the body of the flesh (the whole corrupt, carnal nature with its passions and lusts).

Colossians 2:15 [God] disarmed the principalities and powers that were ranged against us and made a bold display and public example of them, in triumphing over them in Him and in it [the cross].

1 John 2:5 But he who keeps (treasures) His Word [who bears in mind His precepts, who observes His message in its entirety], truly in him has the love of and for God been perfected (completed, reached maturity). By this we may perceive (know, recognize, and be sure) that we are in Him.

1 John 2:6 Whoever says he abides in Him ought [as a personal debt] to walk and conduct himself in the same way in which He walked and conducted Himself.

73

1 John 2:8 Yet I am writing you a new commandment, which is true (is realized) in Him and in you, because the darkness (moral blindness) is clearing away and the true Light (the revelation of God in Christ) is already shining.

1 John 2:27 But as for you, the anointing (the sacred appointment, the unction) which you received from Him abides [permanently] in you; [so] then you have no need that anyone should instruct you. But just as His anointing teaches you concerning everything and is true and is no falsehood, so you must abide in (live in, never depart from) Him [being rooted in Him, knit to Him], just as [His anointing] has taught you [to do].

1 John 2:28 And now, little children, abide (live, remain permanently) in Him, so that when He is made visible, we may have and enjoy perfect confidence (boldness, assurance) and not be ashamed and shrink from Him at His coming.

1 John 3:3 And everyone who has this hope [resting] on Him cleanses (purifies) himself just as He is pure (chaste, undefiled, guiltless).

1 John 3:6 No one who abides in Him [who lives and remains in communion with and in obedience to Him--deliberately, knowingly, and habitually] commits (practices) sin. No one who [habitually] sins has either seen or known Him [recognized, perceived, or understood Him, or has had an experiential acquaintance with Him].

1 John 3:24 All who keep His commandments [who obey His orders and follow His plan, live and continue to live, to stay and] abide in Him, and He in them. [They let Christ be a home to them and they are the home of Christ.] And by this we know and understand and have the proof that He [really] lives and makes His home in us: by the [Holy] Spirit Whom He has given us.

1 John 4:13 By this we come to know (perceive, recognize, and understand) that we abide (live and remain) in Him and He in us: because He has given (imparted) to us of His [Holy] Spirit.

1 John 5:14 And this is the confidence (the assurance, the privilege of boldness) which we have in Him: [we are sure] that if we ask anything (make any request) according to His will (in agreement with His own plan), He listens to and hears us.

1 John 5:15 And if (since) we [positively] know that He listens to us in whatever we ask, we also know [with settled and absolute knowledge] that we have [granted us as our present possessions] the requests made of Him.

1 John 5:20 And we [have seen and] know [positively] that the Son of God has [actually] come to this world and has given us understanding and insight [progressively] to perceive (recognize) and come to know better and more clearly Him Who is true; and we are in Him Who is true–in His Son Jesus Christ (the Messiah). This [Man] is the true God and Life eternal.

1 Peter 1:8 Without having seen Him, you love Him; though you do not [even] now see Him, you believe in Him and exult and thrill with inexpressible and glorious (triumphant, heavenly) joy.

IN THE BELOVED

Ephesians 1:6 [So that we might be] to the praise and the commendation of His glorious grace (favor and mercy), which He so freely bestowed on us in the Beloved.

IN THE LORD

Ephesians 5:8 For once you were darkness, but now you are light in the Lord; walk as children of Light [lead the lives of those native-born to the Light].

Ephesians 6:10 In conclusion, be strong in the Lord [be empowered through your union with Him]; draw your strength from Him [that strength which His boundless might provides].

IN WHOM

Ephesians 3:12 In Whom, because of our faith in Him, we dare to have the boldness (courage and confidence) of free access (an unreserved approach to God with freedom and without fear).

Colossians 1:14 In Whom we have our redemption through His blood, [which means] the forgiveness of our sins.

BY CHRIST

1 Corinthians 7:23 You were bought with a price [purchased with a preciousness and paid for by Christ]; then do not yield yourselves up to become [in your own estimation] slaves to men [but consider yourselves slaves to Christ].

Romans 5:19 For just as by one man's disobedience (failing to hear, heedlessness, and carelessness) the many were constituted sinners, so by one Man's obedience the many will be constituted righteous (made acceptable to God, brought into right standing with Him).

Ephesians 3:9 Also to enlighten all men and make plain to them what is the plan [regarding the Gentiles and providing for the salvation of all men] of the mystery kept hidden through the ages and concealed until now in [the mind of] God Who created all things by Christ Jesus.

1 Peter 1:3 Praised (honored, blessed) be the God and Father of our Lord Jesus Christ (the Messiah)! By His boundless mercy we have been born again to an ever-living hope through the resurrection of Jesus Christ from the dead.

THROUGH CHRIST

Romans 5:1 Therefore, since we are justified (acquitted, declared righteous, and given a right standing with God) through faith, let us [grasp the fact that we] have [the peace of reconciliation to hold and to enjoy] peace with God through our Lord Jesus Christ (the Messiah, the Anointed One).

Romans 5:11 Not only so, but we also rejoice and exultingly glory in God [in His love and perfection] through our Lord Jesus Christ, through Whom we have now received and enjoy [our] reconciliation.

Romans 5:15 But God's free gift is not at all to be compared to the trespass [His grace is out of all proportion to the fall of man]. For if many died through one man's falling away (his lapse, his offense), much more profusely did God's grace and the free gift [that comes] through the undeserved favor of the one Man Jesus Christ abound and overflow to and for [the benefit of] many.

Romans 5:17 For if because of one man's trespass (lapse, offense) death reigned through that one, much more surely will those who receive [God's] overflowing grace (unmerited favor) and the free gift of righteousness [putting them into right standing with Himself] reign as kings in life through the one Man Jesus Christ (the Messiah, the Anointed One).

Romans 6:23 For the wages which sin pays is death, but the [bountiful] free gift of God is eternal life through (in union with) Jesus Christ our Lord.

Romans 7:4 Likewise, my brethren, you have undergone death as to the Law through the [crucified] body of Christ, so that now you may belong to Another, to Him Who was raised from the dead in order that we may bear fruit for God.

1 Corinthians 15:57 But thanks be to God, Who gives us the victory [making us conquerors] through our Lord Jesus Christ.

2 Corinthians 5:18 But all things are from God, Who through Jesus Christ reconciled us to Himself [received us into favor, brought us into harmony with Himself] and gave to us the ministry of reconciliation [that by word and deed we might aim to bring others into harmony with Him].

Galatians 3:14 To the end that through [their receiving] Christ Jesus, the blessing [promised] to Abraham might come upon the Gentiles, so that we through faith might [all] receive [the realization of] the promise of the [Holy] Spirit.

Galatians 4:7 Therefore, you are no longer a slave (bond servant) but a son; and if a son, then [it follows that you are] an heir by the aid of God, through Christ.

Ephesians 1:5 For He foreordained us (destined us, planned in love for us) to be adopted (revealed) as His own children through Jesus Christ, in accordance with the purpose of His will [because it pleased Him and was His kind intent].

Philippians 1:11 May you abound in and be filled with the fruits of righteousness (of right standing with God and right doing) which come through Jesus Christ (the Anointed One), to the honor and praise of God [that His glory may be both manifested and recognized].

Hebrews 13:20-21v. 20 Now may the God of peace [Who is the Author and the Giver of peace], Who brought again from among the dead our Lord Jesus, that great Shepherd of the sheep, by the blood [that sealed, ratified] the everlasting agreement (covenant, testament),v. 21 Strengthen (complete, perfect) and make you what you ought to be and equip you with everything good that you may carry out His will; [while He Himself] works in you and accomplishes that which is pleasing in His sight, through Jesus Christ (the Messiah); to Whom be the glory forever and ever (to the ages of the ages). Amen (so be it).

1 Peter 2:5 [Come] and, like living stones, be yourselves built [into] a spiritual house, for a holy (dedicated, consecrated) priesthood, to offer up [those] spiritual sacrifices [that are] acceptable and pleasing to God through Jesus Christ.

THROUGH HIM

Romans 1:5 It is through Him that we have received grace (God's unmerited favor) and [our] apostleship to promote obedience to the faith and make disciples for His name's sake among all the nations.

Romans 5:2 Through Him also we have [our] access (entrance, introduction) by faith into this grace (state of God's favor) in which we [firmly and safely] stand. And let us rejoice and exult in our hope of experiencing and enjoying the glory of God.

Romans 8:37 Yet amid all these things we are more than conquerors and gain a surpassing victory through Him Who loved us.

Romans 11:36 For from Him and through Him and to Him are all things. [For all things originate with Him and come from Him; all things live through Him, and all things center in and tend to consummate and to end in Him.] To Him be glory forever! Amen (so be it).

Ephesians 2:18 For it is through Him that we both [whether far off or near] now have an introduction (access) by one [Holy] Spirit to the Father [so that we are able to approach Him].

Colossians 1:20 And God purposed that through (by the service, the intervention of) Him [the Son] all things should be completely reconciled back to Himself, whether on earth or in heaven, as through Him, [the Father] made peace by means of the blood of His cross.

Colossians 3:17 And whatever you do [no matter what it is] in word or deed, do everything in the name of the Lord Jesus and in [dependence upon] His Person, giving praise to God the Father through Him.

Hebrews 7:25 Therefore He is able also to save to the uttermost (completely, perfectly, finally, and for all time and eternity) those who come to God through Him, since He is always living to make petition to God and intercede with Him and intervene for them.

Hebrews 13:15 Through Him, therefore, let us constantly and at all times offer up to God a sacrifice of praise, which is the fruit of lips that thankfully acknowledge and confess and glorify His name.

1 Peter 1:21 Through Him you believe in (adhere to, rely on) God, Who raised Him up from the dead and gave Him honor and glory, so that your faith and hope are [centered and rest] in God.

1 John 4:9 In this the love of God was made manifest (displayed) where we are concerned: in that God sent His Son, the only begotten or unique [Son], into the world so that we might live through Him.

BY WHOM

1 Corinthians 8:6 Yet for us there is [only] one God, the Father, Who is the Source of all things and for Whom we [have life], and one Lord, Jesus Christ, through and by Whom are all things and through and by Whom we [ourselves exist].

THROUGH WHOM

2 Corinthians 1:24 Not that we have dominion [over you] and lord it over your faith, but [rather that we work with you as] fellow laborers [to promote] your joy, for in [your] faith (in your strong and welcome conviction or belief that Jesus is the Messiah, through Whom we obtain eternal salvation in the kingdom of God) you stand firm.

Galatians 6:14 But far be it from me to glory [in anything or anyone] except in the cross of our Lord Jesus Christ (the Messiah) through Whom the world has been crucified to me, and I to the world!

Hebrews 1:2 [But] in the last of these days He has spoken to us in [the person of a] Son, Whom He appointed Heir and lawful Owner of all things, also by and through Whom He created the worlds and the reaches of space and the ages of time [He made, produced, built, operated, and arranged them in order].

FROM WHOM

Colossians 2:19 And not holding fast to the Head, from Whom the entire body, supplied and knit together by means of its joints and ligaments, grows with a growth that is from God.

BY HIMSELF

Galatians 3:13 Christ purchased our freedom [redeeming us] from the curse (doom) of the Law [and its condemnation] by [Himself] becoming a curse for us, for it is written [in the Scriptures], Cursed is everyone who hangs on a tree (is crucified).

Hebrews 1:3 He is the sole expression of the glory of God [the Light-being, the out-raying or radiance of the divine], and He is the perfect imprint and very image of [God's] nature, upholding and maintaining and guiding and propelling the universe by His mighty word of power. When He had by offering Himself accomplished our cleansing of sins and riddance of guilt, He sat down at the right hand of the divine Majesty on high.

Hebrews 9:26 For then would He often have had to suffer [over and over again] since the foundation of the world. But as it now is, He has once for all at the consummation and close of the ages appeared to put away and abolish sin by His sacrifice [of Himself].BY HIS BLOOD

Hebrews 9:12 He went once for all into the [Holy of] Holies [of heaven], not by virtue of the blood of goats and calves [by which to make reconciliation between God and man], but His own blood, having found and secured a complete redemption (an everlasting release for us).

Hebrews 10:19 Therefore, brethren, since we have full freedom and confidence to enter into the [Holy of] Holies [by the power and virtue] in the blood of Jesus.

1 John 1:7 But if we [really] are living and walking in the Light, as He [Himself] is in the Light, we have [true, unbroken] fellowship with one another, and the blood of Jesus Christ His Son cleanses (removes) us from all sin and guilt [keeps us cleansed from sin in all its forms and manifestations].

OF CHRIST

Romans 7:4 Likewise, my brethren, you have undergone death as to the Law through the [crucified] body of Christ, so that now you may belong to Another, to Him Who was raised from the dead in order that we may bear fruit for God.

Romans 8:9 But you are not living the life of the flesh, you are living the life of the Spirit, if the [Holy] Spirit of God [really] dwells within you [directs and controls you]. But if anyone does not possess the [Holy] Spirit of Christ, he is none of His [he does not belong to Christ, is not truly a child of God].

Romans 10:17 So faith comes by hearing [what is told], and what is heard comes by the preaching [of the message that came from the lips] of Christ (the Messiah Himself).

1 Corinthians 2:16 For who has known or understood the mind (the counsels and purposes) of the Lord so as to guide and instruct Him and give Him knowledge? But we have the mind of Christ (the Messiah) and do hold the thoughts (feelings and purposes) of His heart.

1 Corinthians 6:15 Do you not see and know that your bodies are members (bodily parts) of Christ (the Messiah)? Am I therefore to take the parts of Christ and make [them] parts of a prostitute? Never! Never!

1 Corinthians 10:16 The cup of blessing [of wine at the Lord's Supper] upon which we ask [God's] blessing, does it not mean [that in drinking it] we participate in and share a fellowship (a communion) in the blood of Christ (the Messiah)? The bread which we break, does it not mean [that in eating it] we participate in and share a fellowship (a communion) in the body of Christ?

2 Corinthians 2:15 For we are the sweet fragrance of Christ [which exhales] unto God, [discernible alike] among those who are being saved and among those who are perishing.

2 Corinthians 5:14 For the love of Christ controls and urges and impels us, because we are of the opinion and conviction that [if] One died for all, then all died.

Ephesians 3:19 [That you may really come] to know [practically, through experience for yourselves] the love of Christ, which far surpasses mere knowledge [without experience]; that you may be filled [through all your being] unto all the fullness of God [may have the richest measure of the divine Presence, and become a body wholly filled and flooded with God Himself]!

Colossians 3:15 And let the peace (soul harmony which comes) from Christ rule (act as umpire continually) in your hearts [deciding and settling with finality all questions that arise in your minds, in that peaceful state] to which as [members of Christ's] one body you were also called [to live]. And be thankful (appreciative), [giving praise to God always].

2 Thessalonians 3:5 May the Lord direct your hearts into [realizing and showing] the love of God and into the steadfastness and patience of Christ and in waiting for His return.

Hebrews 9:14 How much more surely shall the blood of Christ, Who by virtue of [His] eternal Spirit [His own preexistent divine personality] has offered Himself as an unblemished sacrifice to God, purify our consciences from dead works and lifeless observances to serve the [ever] living God?

1 Peter 4:1 So, since Christ suffered in the flesh for us, for you, arm yourselves with the same thought and purpose [patiently to suffer rather than fail to please God]. For whoever has suffered in the flesh [having the mind of Christ] is done with [intentional] sin [has stopped pleasing himself and the world, and pleases God].

2 Peter 1:8 For as these qualities are yours and increasingly abound in you, they will keep [you] from being idle or unfruitful unto the [full personal] knowledge of our Lord Jesus Christ (the Messiah, the Anointed One).

1 John 3:24 All who keep His commandments [who obey His orders and follow His plan, live and continue to live, to stay and] abide in Him, and He in them. [They let Christ be a home to them and they are the home of Christ.] And by this we know and understand and have the proof that He [really] lives and makes His home in us: by the [Holy] Spirit Whom He has given us.

2 John 1:9 Anyone who runs on ahead [of God] and does not abide in the doctrine of Christ [who is not content with what He taught] does not have God; but he who continues to live in the doctrine (teaching) of Christ [does have God], he has both the Father and the Son.

OF HIM

Ephesians 4:16 For because of Him the whole body (the church, in all its various parts), closely joined and firmly knit together by the joints and ligaments with which it is supplied, when each part [with power adapted to its need] is working properly [in all its functions], grows to full maturity, building itself up in love.

FROM HIM

1 John 1:5 And this is the message [the message of promise] which we have heard from Him and now are reporting to you: God is Light, and there is no darkness in Him at all [no, not in any way].

1 John 2:27 But as for you, the anointing (the sacred appointment, the unction) which you received from Him abides [permanently] in you; [so] then you have no need that anyone should instruct you. But just as His anointing teaches you concerning everything and is true and is no falsehood, so you must abide in (live in, never depart from) Him [being rooted in Him, knit to Him], just as [His anointing] has taught you [to do].

FROM WHOM

Colossians 2:19 And not holding fast to the Head, from Whom the entire body, supplied and knit together by means of its joints and ligaments, grows with a growth that is from God.

WITH CHRIST

Romans 6:8 Now if we have died with Christ, we believe that we shall also live with Him.

Galatians 2:20 I have been crucified with Christ [in Him I have shared His crucifixion]; it is no longer I who live, but Christ (the Messiah) lives in me; and the life I now live in the body I live by faith in (by adherence to and reliance on and complete trust in) the Son of God, Who loved me and gave Himself up for me.

Ephesians 2:5 Even when we were dead (slain) by [our own] shortcomings and trespasses, He made us alive together in fellowship and in union with Christ; [He gave us the very life of Christ Himself, the same new life with which He quickened Him, for] it is by grace (His favor and mercy which you did not deserve) that you are saved (delivered from judgment and made partakers of Christ's salvation).

Colossians 2:13 And you who were dead in trespasses and in the uncircumcision of your flesh (your sensuality, your sinful carnal nature), [God] brought to life together with [Christ], having [freely] forgiven us all our transgressions.

Colossians 2:20 If then you have died with Christ to material ways of looking at things and have escaped from the world's crude and elemental notions and teachings of externalism, why do you live as if you still belong to the world? [Why do you submit to rules and regulations?-such as]

Colossians 3:1 If then you have been raised with Christ [to a new life, thus sharing His resurrection from the dead], aim at and seek the [rich, eternal treasures] that are above, where Christ is, seated at the right hand of God.

Colossians 3:3 For [as far as this world is concerned] you have died, and your [new, real] life is hidden with Christ in God.

WITH HIM

Romans 6:4 We were buried therefore with Him by the baptism into death, so that just as Christ was raised from the dead by the glorious [power] of the Father, so we too might [habitually] live and behave in newness of life.

Romans 6:6 We know that our old (un-renewed) self was nailed to the cross with Him in order that [our] body [which is the instrument] of sin might be made ineffective and inactive for evil, that we might no longer be the slaves of sin.

Romans 6:8 Now if we have died with Christ, we believe that we shall also live with Him.

Romans 8:32 He who did not withhold or spare [even] His own Son but gave Him up for us all, will He not also with Him freely and graciously give us all [other] things?

2 Corinthians 13:4 For though He was crucified in weakness, yet He goes on living by the power of God. And though we too are weak in Him [as He was humanly weak], yet in dealing with you [we shall show ourselves] alive and strong in [fellowship with] Him by the power of God.

Colossians 2:12[Thus you were circumcised when] you were buried with Him in [your] baptism, in which you were also raised with Him [to a new life] through [your] faith in the working of God [as displayed] when He raised Him up from the dead.

Colossians 3:4 When Christ, Who is our life, appears, then you also will appear with Him in [the splendor of His] glory.

2 Timothy 2:11 The saying is sure and worthy of confidence: If we have died with Him, we shall also live with Him.

2 Timothy 2:12 If we endure, we shall also reign with Him. If we deny and disown and reject Him, He will also deny and disown and reject us.

IN ME

Acts 26:18 To open their eyes that they may turn from darkness to light and from the power of Satan to God, so that they may thus receive forgiveness and release from their sins and a place and portion among those who are consecrated and purified by faith in Me.

IN MY (HIS) NAME

1 Corinthians 6:11 And such some of you were [once]. But you were washed clean (purified by a complete atonement for sin and made free from the guilt of sin), and you were consecrated (set apart, hallowed), and you were justified [pronounced righteous, by trusting] in the name of the Lord Jesus Christ and in the [Holy] Spirit of our God.

82

Appendix 3
Resources for Further Growth

Books

The Purpose Driven Life by Rick Warren

Experiencing God by Henry Blackaby

God's Promises for You by Max Lucado

So, You Want to be Like Christ by Chuck Swindoll

Web Sites

www.BibleGateway.com—Read the Bible online

www.calvaryfi.com—Click on resource header.

Appendix 4
Calvary Fellowship International's
Statement of Beliefs

1. About God

God is the Creator and Ruler of the universe. He has eternally existed in three personalities: the Father, the Son, and the Holy Spirit. These three are coequal and are one God. Genesis 1:1, 26, 27; 3:22 || Psalm 90:2 || Matthew 28:19 || 1 Peter 1:2 || 2 Corinthians 13:14

2. About You

You are made in the spiritual image of God to be like Him in character. You are the supreme object of God's creation and love. Although you have tremendous potential for good, you are marred by an attitude of disobedience toward God called *sin*. This attitude separates you from God until the relationship is restored through a personal commitment to following Jesus Christ as your personal Lord and Savior. Genesis 1:27 || Psalms 8:3–6 || Isaiah 53:6 || Romans 3:23 || Isaiah 59: 1–2

3. About Eternity

Humans were created to exist forever. We will either exist eternally separated from God by sin or in union with God through forgiveness and salvation. To be eternally separated from God is Hell. To be eternally in union with Him is eternal life. Heaven and Hell are places of eternal existence. John 3:16 || 1 John 2:25; 5:11-13 || Romans 6:23 || Revelation 20:15

4. About Jesus Christ

Jesus Christ is the Son of God. He is coequal with the Father. Jesus lived a sinless human life and offered Himself as the perfect sacrifice for the sins of all people by dying on a cross. He rose from the dead after three days to demonstrate His power over sin and death. He ascended to Heaven's glory and will return again to earth to reign as King of Kings, and Lord of Lords. Matthew 1:22–23 || Isaiah 9:6 || John 1:1-5; 14:10–30 || Hebrews 4:14-15 || 1 Corinthians 15: 3–4 || Romans 1:3–4 Acts 1:9-11 || 2 Timothy 6:14–15 || Titus 2:13

5. About Salvation

Salvation is a gift from God to humanity. We can never make up for our sin by self-improvement or good works. Only by trusting in Jesus Christ as God's offer of forgiveness can we be saved from sin's penalty. Eternal life begins the moment one receives Jesus Christ into his life by faith. Romans 6:23 || Ephesians 2:8–9 || John 14:6; 1:12 || Titus 3:5 || Galatians 3:26 || Romans 5:1

6. About Eternal Security

Because God gives us eternal life through Jesus Christ, the believer is secure in that salvation for eternity. Salvation is maintained by the grace of God and the power of God, not by the self-effort of the Christian. It is grace and the keeping power of God that gives us this security. John 10:29 || 2I Timothy 1:12 || Hebrews 7:25; 10:10-14 || 1 Peter 1:3–5

7. About the Holy Spirit

The Holy Spirit is equal with the Father and the Son as God. He is present in the world to make people aware of their need for Jesus Christ. He also lives in every Christian from the moment of salvation. There are two experiences that the New Testament teaches in regards to the Holy Spirit. The Spirit of God within us for salvation and The Spirit of God upon us for service and power. This latter experience is called the Baptism with the Holy Spirit (Cp. Acts 1:5). All believers are entitled to the Baptism with the Holy Spirit and Fire, according to the command of our Lord Jesus

Christ. With it comes the endowment of power for service, the bestowment of the spiritual gifts and their uses in the work of the ministry. Luke 24:49 || Acts 1:4-8 || 1 Cor. 12:1-3 || 2 Corinthians 3:17 || John 16:7-13; 14:16–17 || Acts 1:8 || 2 Corinthians 2:12; 3:16 || Ephesians 1:13 Galatians 5:25 || Ephesians 5:18

This wonderful experience is distinct from and subsequent to the experience of the new birth. Acts 2:38 || 10:44-46 || 11:14-16 || 15:7-9 || 19:1-6

The full consummation of the Baptism of believers with the Holy Spirit is evidenced by the initial physical sign of speaking with other tongues as the Spirit gives utterance, and by the subsequent manifestation of spiritual power in public testimony and service. Acts 1:8 || 2:4 || 10:44-46 || 19:2-6 || 1 Corinthians 12:1-11 || 2 Corinthians 3:17 || John 16:7-13; 14:16–17 || Acts 1:8 || 2 Corinthians 2:12; 3:16 || Ephesians 1:13 Galatians 5:25 || Ephesians 5:18

8. About the Bible

The Bible is God's Word to all people. It was written through human authors under the supernatural guidance of the Holy Spirit. It is the supreme source of truth for Christian beliefs and living. Because it is God inspired or God breathed, it is truth without any mixture of error. 2 Timothy 3:16 || 2 Peter 1:20–21 || 2 Timothy 1:13 || Psalms 119:105, 160; 12:6 || Proverbs 30

Reading Plan for the Gospel of John

- ☐ Day 1: John 1–7
- ☐ Day 2: John 8–14
- ☐ Day 3: John 15–21
- ☐ Day 4: John 1:1–18
- ☐ Day 5: John 1:19–51
- ☐ Day 6: John 2:1–25
- ☐ Day 7: John 3:1–36
- ☐ Day 8: John 4:1–38
- ☐ Day 9: John 4:39–5:15
- ☐ Day 10: John 5:16–47
- ☐ Day 11: John 6:1–21
- ☐ Day 12: John 6:22–71
- ☐ Day 13: John 7:1–36
- ☐ Day 14: John 7:37–8:11
- ☐ Day 15: John 8:12–30
- ☐ Day 16: John 8:31–59
- ☐ Day 17: John 9:1–34
- ☐ Day 18: John 9:35–10:21
- ☐ Day 18: John 10:22–42
- ☐ Day 19: John 11:1–44
- ☐ Day 20: John 11:45–12:19
- ☐ Day 21: John 12:20–50
- ☐ Day 22: John 13:1–38
- ☐ Day 23: John 14:1–31
- ☐ Day 24: John 15:1–27
- ☐ Day 25: John 16:1–33
- ☐ Day 26: John 17:1–26
- ☐ Day 27: John 18:1–27

- ☐ Day 28: John 18:28–19:16
- ☐ Day 29: John 19:17–42
- ☐ Day 30: John 20:1–23
- ☐ Day 31: John 20:24–31
- ☐ Day 32: John 21:1–25

The Gospel of John

Chapter 1

Prologue: Christ, the Eternal Word
 [1] In the beginning the Word already existed.
   The Word was with God,
   and the Word was God.
 [2] He existed in the beginning with God.
 [3] God created everything through him,
   and nothing was created except through him.
 [4] The Word gave life to everything that was created,
   and his life brought light to everyone.
 [5] The light shines in the darkness,
   and the darkness can never extinguish it.

[6] God sent a man, John the Baptist, [7] to tell about the light so that everyone might believe because of his testimony. [8] John himself was not the light; he was simply a witness to tell about the light. [9] The one who is the true light, who gives light to everyone, was coming into the world.

[10] He came into the very world he created, but the world didn't recognize him. [11] He came to his own people, and even they rejected him. [12] But to all who believed him and accepted him, he gave the right to become children of God. [13] They are reborn—not with a physical birth resulting from human passion or plan, but a birth that comes from God.

[14] So the Word became human and made his home among us. He was full of unfailing love and faithfulness. And we have seen his glory, the glory of the Father's one and only Son.

[15] John testified about him when he shouted to the crowds, "This is the one I was talking about when I said, 'Someone is coming after me who is far greater than I am, for he existed long before me.' "

[16] From his abundance we have all received one gracious blessing after another. [17] For the law was given through Moses, but God's unfailing love and

faithfulness came through Jesus Christ. [18] No one has ever seen God. But the unique One, who is himself God, is near to the Father's heart. He has revealed God to us.

The Testimony of John the Baptist

[19] This was John's testimony when the Jewish leaders sent priests and Temple assistants from Jerusalem to ask John, "Who are you?" [20] He came right out and said, "I am not the Messiah."

[21] "Well then, who are you?" they asked. "Are you Elijah?"

"No," he replied.

"Are you the Prophet we are expecting?"

"No."

[22] "Then who are you? We need an answer for those who sent us. What do you have to say about yourself?"

[23] John replied in the words of the prophet Isaiah:

"I am a voice shouting in the wilderness,
'Clear the way for the LORD's coming!' "

[24] Then the Pharisees who had been sent [25] asked him, "If you aren't the Messiah or Elijah or the Prophet, what right do you have to baptize?"

[26] John told them, "I baptize with water, but right here in the crowd is someone you do not recognize. [27] Though his ministry follows mine, I'm not even worthy to be his slave and untie the straps of his sandal."

[28] This encounter took place in Bethany, an area east of the Jordan River, where John was baptizing.

Jesus, the Lamb of God

[29] The next day John saw Jesus coming toward him and said, "Look! The Lamb of God who takes away the sin of the world! [30] He is the one I was talking about when I said, 'A man is coming after me who is far greater than I am, for he existed long before me.' [31] I did not recognize him as the Messiah, but I have been baptizing with water so that he might be revealed to Israel."

[32] Then John testified, "I saw the Holy Spirit descending like a dove from heaven and resting upon him. [33] I didn't know he was the one, but when God sent me to baptize with water, he told me, 'The one on whom you see the Spirit descend and rest is the one who will baptize with the Holy Spirit.' [34] I saw this happen to Jesus, so I testify that he is the Chosen One of God."

The First Disciples

[35] The following day John was again standing with two of his disciples. [36] As Jesus walked by, John looked at him and declared, "Look! There is the Lamb of God!" [37] When John's two disciples heard this, they followed Jesus.

[38] Jesus looked around and saw them following. "What do you want?" he asked them.

They replied, "Rabbi" (which means "Teacher"), "where are you staying?"

[39] "Come and see," he said. It was about four o'clock in the afternoon when they went with him to the place where he was staying, and they remained with him the rest of the day.

[40] Andrew, Simon Peter's brother, was one of these men who heard what John said and then followed Jesus. [41] Andrew went to find his brother, Simon, and told him, "We have found the Messiah" (which means "Christ").

[42] Then Andrew brought Simon to meet Jesus. Looking intently at Simon, Jesus said, "Your name is Simon, son of John—but you will be called Cephas" (which means "Peter").

[43] The next day Jesus decided to go to Galilee. He found Philip and said to him, "Come, follow me." [44] Philip was from Bethsaida, Andrew and Peter's hometown.

[45] Philip went to look for Nathanael and told him, "We have found the very person Moses and the prophets wrote about! His name is Jesus, the son of Joseph from Nazareth."

[46] "Nazareth!" exclaimed Nathanael. "Can anything good come from Nazareth?"

"Come and see for yourself," Philip replied.

[47] As they approached, Jesus said, "Now here is a genuine son of Israel—a man of complete integrity."

[48] "How do you know about me?" Nathanael asked.

Jesus replied, "I could see you under the fig tree before Philip found you."

[49] Then Nathanael exclaimed, "Rabbi, you are the Son of God—the King of Israel!"

[50] Jesus asked him, "Do you believe this just because I told you I had seen you under the fig tree? You will see greater things than this." [51] Then he said, "I tell you the truth, you will all see heaven open and the angels of God going up and down on the Son of Man, the one who is the stairway between heaven and earth."

Chapter 2

The Wedding at Cana

The next day there was a wedding celebration in the village of Cana in Galilee. Jesus' mother was there, [2] and Jesus and his disciples were also invited to the celebration. [3] The wine supply ran out during the festivities, so Jesus' mother told him, "They have no more wine."

[4] "Dear woman, that's not our problem," Jesus replied. "My time has not yet come."

[5] But his mother told the servants, "Do whatever he tells you."

[6] Standing nearby were six stone water jars, used for Jewish ceremonial washing. Each could hold twenty to thirty gallons. [7] Jesus told the servants, "Fill the jars with water." When the jars had been filled, [8] he said, "Now dip some out, and take it to the master of ceremonies." So the servants followed his instructions.

[9] When the master of ceremonies tasted the water that was now wine, not knowing where it had come from (though, of course, the servants knew), he called the bridegroom over. [10] "A host always serves the best wine first," he said. "Then, when everyone has had a lot to drink, he brings out the less expensive wine. But you have kept the best until now!"

[11] This miraculous sign at Cana in Galilee was the first time Jesus revealed his glory. And his disciples believed in him.

[12] After the wedding he went to Capernaum for a few days with his mother, his brothers, and his disciples.

Jesus Clears the Temple

[13] It was nearly time for the Jewish Passover celebration, so Jesus went to Jerusalem. [14] In the Temple area he saw merchants selling cattle, sheep, and doves for sacrifices; he also saw dealers at tables exchanging foreign money. [15] Jesus made a whip from some ropes and chased them all out of the Temple. He drove out the sheep and cattle, scattered the money changers' coins over the floor, and turned over their tables. [16] Then, going over to the people who sold doves, he told them, "Get these things out of here. Stop turning my Father's house into a marketplace!"

[17] Then his disciples remembered this prophecy from the Scriptures: "Passion for God's house will consume me."

[18] But the Jewish leaders demanded, "What are you doing? If God gave you authority to do this, show us a miraculous sign to prove it."

¹⁹ "All right," Jesus replied. "Destroy this temple, and in three days I will raise it up."

²⁰ "What!" they exclaimed. "It has taken forty-six years to build this Temple, and you can rebuild it in three days?" ²¹ But when Jesus said "this temple," he meant his own body. ²² After he was raised from the dead, his disciples remembered he had said this, and they believed both the Scriptures and what Jesus had said.

Jesus and Nicodemus

²³ Because of the miraculous signs Jesus did in Jerusalem at the Passover celebration, many began to trust in him. ²⁴ But Jesus didn't trust them, because he knew human nature. ²⁵ No one needed to tell him what mankind is really like.

Chapter 3

There was a man named Nicodemus, a Jewish religious leader who was a Pharisee. ² After dark one evening, he came to speak with Jesus. "Rabbi," he said, "we all know that God has sent you to teach us. Your miraculous signs are evidence that God is with you."

³ Jesus replied, "I tell you the truth, unless you are born again, you cannot see the Kingdom of God."

⁴ "What do you mean?" exclaimed Nicodemus. "How can an old man go back into his mother's womb and be born again?"

⁵ Jesus replied, "I assure you, no one can enter the Kingdom of God without being born of water and the Spirit. ⁶ Humans can reproduce only human life, but the Holy Spirit gives birth to spiritual life. ⁷ So don't be surprised when I say, 'You must be born again.' ⁸ The wind blows wherever it wants. Just as you can hear the wind but can't tell where it comes from or where it is going, so you can't explain how people are born of the Spirit."

⁹ "How are these things possible?" Nicodemus asked.

¹⁰ Jesus replied, "You are a respected Jewish teacher, and yet you don't understand these things? ¹¹ I assure you, we tell you what we know and have seen, and yet you won't believe our testimony. ¹² But if you don't believe me when I tell you about earthly things, how can you possibly believe if I tell you about heavenly things? ¹³ No one has ever gone to heaven and returned. But the Son of Man has come down from heaven. ¹⁴ And as Moses lifted up the bronze snake on a pole in the wilderness, so the Son of Man must be lifted up,

[15] so that everyone who believes in him will have eternal life.

[16] "For God loved the world so much that he gave his one and only Son, so that everyone who believes in him will not perish but have eternal life. [17] God sent his Son into the world not to judge the world, but to save the world through him.

[18] "There is no judgment against anyone who believes in him. But anyone who does not believe in him has already been judged for not believing in God's one and only Son. [19] And the judgment is based on this fact: God's light came into the world, but people loved the darkness more than the light, for their actions were evil. [20] All who do evil hate the light and refuse to go near it for fear their sins will be exposed. [21] But those who do what is right come to the light so others can see that they are doing what God wants."

John the Baptist Exalts Jesus

[22] Then Jesus and his disciples left Jerusalem and went into the Judean countryside. Jesus spent some time with them there, baptizing people.

[23] At this time John the Baptist was baptizing at Aenon, near Salim, because there was plenty of water there; and people kept coming to him for baptism. [24] (This was before John was thrown into prison.) [25] A debate broke out between John's disciples and a certain Jew over ceremonial cleansing. [26] So John's disciples came to him and said, "Rabbi, the man you met on the other side of the Jordan River, the one you identified as the Messiah, is also baptizing people. And everybody is going to him instead of coming to us."

[27] John replied, "No one can receive anything unless God gives it from heaven. [28] You yourselves know how plainly I told you, 'I am not the Messiah. I am only here to prepare the way for him.' [29] It is the bridegroom who marries the bride, and the best man is simply glad to stand with him and hear his vows. Therefore, I am filled with joy at his success. [30] He must become greater and greater, and I must become less and less.

[31] "He has come from above and is greater than anyone else. We are of the earth, and we speak of earthly things, but he has come from heaven and is greater than anyone else. [32] He testifies about what he has seen and heard, but how few believe what he tells them! [33] Anyone who accepts his testimony can affirm that God is true. [34] For he is sent by God. He speaks God's words, for God gives him the Spirit without limit. [35] The Father loves his Son and has put everything into his hands. [36] And anyone who believes in God's Son has eternal life. Anyone who doesn't obey the Son will never experience eternal life but remains under God's angry judgment."

Chapter 4

Jesus and the Samaritan Woman

Jesus knew the Pharisees had heard that he was baptizing and making more disciples than John [2] (though Jesus himself didn't baptize them—his disciples did). [3] So he left Judea and returned to Galilee.

[4] He had to go through Samaria on the way. [5] Eventually he came to the Samaritan village of Sychar, near the field that Jacob gave to his son Joseph. [6] Jacob's well was there; and Jesus, tired from the long walk, sat wearily beside the well about noontime. [7] Soon a Samaritan woman came to draw water, and Jesus said to her, "Please give me a drink." [8] He was alone at the time because his disciples had gone into the village to buy some food.

[9] The woman was surprised, for Jews refuse to have anything to do with Samaritans. She said to Jesus, "You are a Jew, and I am a Samaritan woman. Why are you asking me for a drink?"

[10] Jesus replied, "If you only knew the gift God has for you and who you are speaking to, you would ask me, and I would give you living water."

[11] "But sir, you don't have a rope or a bucket," she said, "and this well is very deep. Where would you get this living water? [12] And besides, do you think you're greater than our ancestor Jacob, who gave us this well? How can you offer better water than he and his sons and his animals enjoyed?"

[13] Jesus replied, "Anyone who drinks this water will soon become thirsty again. [14] But those who drink the water I give will never be thirsty again. It becomes a fresh, bubbling spring within them, giving them eternal life."

[15] "Please, sir," the woman said, "give me this water! Then I'll never be thirsty again, and I won't have to come here to get water."

[16] "Go and get your husband," Jesus told her.

[17] "I don't have a husband," the woman replied.

Jesus said, "You're right! You don't have a husband—[18] for you have had five husbands, and you aren't even married to the man you're living with now. You certainly spoke the truth!"

[19] "Sir," the woman said, "you must be a prophet. [20] So tell me, why is it that you Jews insist that Jerusalem is the only place of worship, while we Samaritans claim it is here at Mount Gerizim, where our ancestors worshiped?"

[21] Jesus replied, "Believe me, dear woman, the time is coming when it will no longer matter whether you worship the Father on this mountain or in Jerusalem. [22] You Samaritans know very little about the one you worship,

while we Jews know all about him, for salvation comes through the Jews.
^{23} But the time is coming—indeed it's here now—when true worshipers will worship the Father in spirit and in truth. The Father is looking for those who will worship him that way. ^{24} For God is Spirit, so those who worship him must worship in spirit and in truth."

^{25} The woman said, "I know the Messiah is coming—the one who is called Christ. When he comes, he will explain everything to us."

^{26} Then Jesus told her, "I AM the Messiah!"

^{27} Just then his disciples came back. They were shocked to find him talking to a woman, but none of them had the nerve to ask, "What do you want with her?" or "Why are you talking to her?" ^{28} The woman left her water jar beside the well and ran back to the village, telling everyone, ^{29} "Come and see a man who told me everything I ever did! Could he possibly be the Messiah?" ^{30} So the people came streaming from the village to see him.

^{31} Meanwhile, the disciples were urging Jesus, "Rabbi, eat something."

^{32} But Jesus replied, "I have a kind of food you know nothing about."

^{33} "Did someone bring him food while we were gone?" the disciples asked each other.

^{34} Then Jesus explained: "My nourishment comes from doing the will of God, who sent me, and from finishing his work. ^{35} You know the saying, 'Four months between planting and harvest.' But I say, wake up and look around. The fields are already ripe for harvest. ^{36} The harvesters are paid good wages, and the fruit they harvest is people brought to eternal life. What joy awaits both the planter and the harvester alike! ^{37} You know the saying, 'One plants and another harvests.' And it's true. ^{38} I sent you to harvest where you didn't plant; others had already done the work, and now you will get to gather the harvest."

Many Samaritans Believe

^{39} Many Samaritans from the village believed in Jesus because the woman had said, "He told me everything I ever did!" ^{40} When they came out to see him, they begged him to stay in their village. So he stayed for two days, ^{41} long enough for many more to hear his message and believe. ^{42} Then they said to the woman, "Now we believe, not just because of what you told us, but because we have heard him ourselves. Now we know that he is indeed the Savior of the world."

Jesus Heals an Official's Son

^{43} At the end of the two days, Jesus went on to Galilee. ^{44} He himself had said that a prophet is not honored in his own hometown. ^{45} Yet the Galileans welcomed him, for they had been in Jerusalem at the Passover celebration and had seen everything he did there.

^{46} As he traveled through Galilee, he came to Cana, where he had turned the water into wine. There was a government official in nearby Capernaum whose son was very sick. ^{47} When he heard that Jesus had come from Judea to Galilee, he went and begged Jesus to come to Capernaum to heal his son, who was about to die.

^{48} Jesus asked, "Will you never believe in me unless you see miraculous signs and wonders?"

^{49} The official pleaded, "Lord, please come now before my little boy dies."

^{50} Then Jesus told him, "Go back home. Your son will live!" And the man believed what Jesus said and started home.

^{51} While the man was on his way, some of his servants met him with the news that his son was alive and well. ^{52} He asked them when the boy had begun to get better, and they replied, "Yesterday afternoon at one o'clock his fever suddenly disappeared!" ^{53} Then the father realized that that was the very time Jesus had told him, "Your son will live." And he and his entire household believed in Jesus. ^{54} This was the second miraculous sign Jesus did in Galilee after coming from Judea.

Chapter 5

Jesus Heals a Lame Man

Afterward Jesus returned to Jerusalem for one of the Jewish holy days. ^{2} Inside the city, near the Sheep Gate, was the pool of Bethesda, with five covered porches. ^{3} Crowds of sick people—blind, lame, or paralyzed—lay on the porches. ^{5} One of the men lying there had been sick for thirty-eight years. ^{6} When Jesus saw him and knew he had been ill for a long time, he asked him, "Would you like to get well?"

^{7} "I can't, sir," the sick man said, "for I have no one to put me into the pool when the water bubbles up. Someone else always gets there ahead of me."

^{8} Jesus told him, "Stand up, pick up your mat, and walk!"

^{9} Instantly, the man was healed! He rolled up his sleeping mat and began walking! But this miracle happened on the Sabbath, ^{10} so the Jewish leaders objected. They said to the man who was cured, "You can't work on the Sabbath! The law doesn't allow you to carry that sleeping mat!"

¹¹ But he replied, "The man who healed me told me, 'Pick up your mat and walk.' "

¹² "Who said such a thing as that?" they demanded.

¹³ The man didn't know, for Jesus had disappeared into the crowd. ¹⁴ But afterward Jesus found him in the Temple and told him, "Now you are well; so stop sinning, or something even worse may happen to you." ¹⁵ Then the man went and told the Jewish leaders that it was Jesus who had healed him.

Jesus Claims to Be the Son of God

¹⁶ So the Jewish leaders began harassing Jesus for breaking the Sabbath rules. ¹⁷ But Jesus replied, "My Father is always working, and so am I." ¹⁸ So the Jewish leaders tried all the harder to find a way to kill him. For he not only broke the Sabbath, he called God his Father, thereby making himself equal with God.

¹⁹ So Jesus explained, "I tell you the truth, the Son can do nothing by himself. He does only what he sees the Father doing. Whatever the Father does, the Son also does. ²⁰ For the Father loves the Son and shows him everything he is doing. In fact, the Father will show him how to do even greater works than healing this man. Then you will truly be astonished. ²¹ For just as the Father gives life to those he raises from the dead, so the Son gives life to anyone he wants. ²² In addition, the Father judges no one. Instead, he has given the Son absolute authority to judge, ²³ so that everyone will honor the Son, just as they honor the Father. Anyone who does not honor the Son is certainly not honoring the Father who sent him.

²⁴ "I tell you the truth, those who listen to my message and believe in God who sent me have eternal life. They will never be condemned for their sins, but they have already passed from death into life.

²⁵ "And I assure you that the time is coming, indeed it's here now, when the dead will hear my voice—the voice of the Son of God. And those who listen will live. ²⁶ The Father has life in himself, and he has granted that same life-giving power to his Son. ²⁷ And he has given him authority to judge everyone because he is the Son of Man. ²⁸ Don't be so surprised! Indeed, the time is coming when all the dead in their graves will hear the voice of God's Son, ²⁹ and they will rise again. Those who have done good will rise to experience eternal life, and those who have continued in evil will rise to experience judgment. ³⁰ I can do nothing on my own. I judge as God tells me.

Therefore, my judgment is just, because I carry out the will of the one who sent me, not my own will.

Witnesses to Jesus

[31] "If I were to testify on my own behalf, my testimony would not be valid. [32] But someone else is also testifying about me, and I assure you that everything he says about me is true. [33] In fact, you sent investigators to listen to John the Baptist, and his testimony about me was true. [34] Of course, I have no need of human witnesses, but I say these things so you might be saved. [35] John was like a burning and shining lamp, and you were excited for a while about his message. [36] But I have a greater witness than John—my teachings and my miracles. The Father gave me these works to accomplish, and they prove that he sent me. [37] And the Father who sent me has testified about me himself. You have never heard his voice or seen him face to face, [38] and you do not have his message in your hearts, because you do not believe me—the one he sent to you.

[39] "You search the Scriptures because you think they give you eternal life. But the Scriptures point to me! [40] Yet you refuse to come to me to receive this life.

[41] "Your approval means nothing to me, [42] because I know you don't have God's love within you. [43] For I have come to you in my Father's name, and you have rejected me. Yet if others come in their own name, you gladly welcome them. [44] No wonder you can't believe! For you gladly honor each other, but you don't care about the honor that comes from the one who alone is God.

[45] "Yet it isn't I who will accuse you before the Father. Moses will accuse you! Yes, Moses, in whom you put your hopes. [46] If you really believed Moses, you would believe me, because he wrote about me. [47] But since you don't believe what he wrote, how will you believe what I say?"

Chapter 6

Jesus Feeds Five Thousand

After this, Jesus crossed over to the far side of the Sea of Galilee, also known as the Sea of Tiberias. [2] A huge crowd kept following him wherever he went, because they saw his miraculous signs as he healed the sick. [3] Then Jesus climbed a hill and sat down with his disciples around him. [4] (It was nearly time for the Jewish Passover celebration.) [5] Jesus soon saw a huge crowd of people coming to look for him. Turning to Philip, he asked, "Where can we buy bread to feed all these people?" [6] He was testing Philip, for he already knew what he was going to do.

[7] Philip replied, "Even if we worked for months, we wouldn't have enough money to feed them!"

[8] Then Andrew, Simon Peter's brother, spoke up. [9] "There's a young boy here with five barley loaves and two fish. But what good is that with this huge crowd?"

[10] "Tell everyone to sit down," Jesus said. So they all sat down on the grassy slopes. (The men alone numbered about 5,000.) [11] Then Jesus took the loaves, gave thanks to God, and distributed them to the people. Afterward he did the same with the fish. And they all ate as much as they wanted. [12] After everyone was full, Jesus told his disciples, "Now gather the leftovers, so that nothing is wasted." [13] So they picked up the pieces and filled twelve baskets with scraps left by the people who had eaten from the five barley loaves.

[14] When the people saw him do this miraculous sign, they exclaimed, "Surely, he is the Prophet we have been expecting!" [15] When Jesus saw that they were ready to force him to be their king, he slipped away into the hills by himself.

Jesus Walks on Water

[16] That evening Jesus' disciples went down to the shore to wait for him. [17] But as darkness fell and Jesus still hadn't come back, they got into the boat and headed across the lake toward Capernaum. [18] Soon a gale swept down upon them, and the sea grew very rough. [19] They had rowed three or four miles when suddenly they saw Jesus walking on the water toward the boat. They were terrified, [20] but he called out to them, "Don't be afraid. I am here!" [21] Then they were eager to let him in the boat, and immediately they arrived at their destination!

Jesus, the Bread of Life

[22] The next day the crowd that had stayed on the far shore saw that the disciples had taken the only boat, and they realized Jesus had not gone with them. [23] Several boats from Tiberias landed near the place where the Lord had blessed the bread and the people had eaten. [24] So when the crowd saw that neither Jesus nor his disciples were there, they got into the boats and went across to Capernaum to look for him. [25] They found him on the other side of the lake and asked, "Rabbi, when did you get here?"

[26] Jesus replied, "I tell you the truth, you want to be with me because I fed you, not because you understood the miraculous signs. [27] But don't be so concerned about perishable things like food. Spend your energy seeking the eternal life that the Son of Man can give you. For God the Father has given me the seal of his approval."

[28] They replied, "We want to perform God's works, too. What should we do?"

[29] Jesus told them, "This is the only work God wants from you: Believe in the one he has sent."

[30] They answered, "Show us a miraculous sign if you want us to believe in you. What can you do? [31] After all, our ancestors ate manna while they journeyed through the wilderness! The Scriptures say, 'Moses gave them bread from heaven to eat.'"

[32] Jesus said, "I tell you the truth, Moses didn't give you bread from heaven. My Father did. And now he offers you the true bread from heaven. [33] The true bread of God is the one who comes down from heaven and gives life to the world."

[34] "Sir," they said, "give us that bread every day."

[35] Jesus replied, "I am the bread of life. Whoever comes to me will never be hungry again. Whoever believes in me will never be thirsty. [36] But you haven't believed in me even though you have seen me. [37] However, those the Father has given me will come to me, and I will never reject them. [38] For I have come down from heaven to do the will of God who sent me, not to do my own will. [39] And this is the will of God, that I should not lose even one of all those he has given me, but that I should raise them up at the last day. [40] For it is my Father's will that all who see his Son and believe in him should have eternal life. I will raise them up at the last day."

[41] Then the people began to murmur in disagreement because he had said, "I am the bread that came down from heaven." [42] They said, "Isn't this Jesus, the son of Joseph? We know his father and mother. How can he say, 'I came down from heaven'?"

[43] But Jesus replied, "Stop complaining about what I said. [44] For no one can come to me unless the Father who sent me draws them to me, and at the last day I will raise them up. [45] As it is written in the Scriptures, 'They will all be taught by God.' Everyone who listens to the Father and learns from him comes to me. [46] (Not that anyone has ever seen the Father; only I, who was sent from God, have seen him.)

⁴⁷ "I tell you the truth, anyone who believes has eternal life. ⁴⁸ Yes, I am the bread of life! ⁴⁹ Your ancestors ate manna in the wilderness, but they all died. ⁵⁰ Anyone who eats the bread from heaven, however, will never die. ⁵¹ I am the living bread that came down from heaven. Anyone who eats this bread will live forever; and this bread, which I will offer so the world may live, is my flesh."

⁵² Then the people began arguing with each other about what he meant. "How can this man give us his flesh to eat?" they asked.

⁵³ So Jesus said again, "I tell you the truth, unless you eat the flesh of the Son of Man and drink his blood, you cannot have eternal life within you. ⁵⁴ But anyone who eats my flesh and drinks my blood has eternal life, and I will raise that person at the last day. ⁵⁵ For my flesh is true food, and my blood is true drink. ⁵⁶ Anyone who eats my flesh and drinks my blood remains in me, and I in him. ⁵⁷ I live because of the living Father who sent me; in the same way, anyone who feeds on me will live because of me. ⁵⁸ I am the true bread that came down from heaven. Anyone who eats this bread will not die as your ancestors did (even though they ate the manna) but will live forever."

⁵⁹ He said these things while he was teaching in the synagogue in Capernaum.

Many Disciples Desert Jesus

⁶⁰ Many of his disciples said, "This is very hard to understand. How can anyone accept it?"

⁶¹ Jesus was aware that his disciples were complaining, so he said to them, "Does this offend you? ⁶² Then what will you think if you see the Son of Man ascend to heaven again? ⁶³ The Spirit alone gives eternal life. Human effort accomplishes nothing. And the very words I have spoken to you are spirit and life. ⁶⁴ But some of you do not believe me." (For Jesus knew from the beginning which ones didn't believe, and he knew who would betray him.) ⁶⁵ Then he said, "That is why I said that people can't come to me unless the Father gives them to me."

⁶⁶ At this point many of his disciples turned away and deserted him. ⁶⁷ Then Jesus turned to the Twelve and asked, "Are you also going to leave?"

⁶⁸ Simon Peter replied, "Lord, to whom would we go? You have the words that give eternal life. ⁶⁹ We believe, and we know you are the Holy One of God."

⁷⁰ Then Jesus said, "I chose the twelve of you, but one is a devil." ⁷¹ He was speaking of Judas, son of Simon Iscariot, one of the Twelve, who would

later betray him.

Chapter 7

Jesus and His Brothers
After this, Jesus traveled around Galilee. He wanted to stay out of Judea, where the Jewish leaders were plotting his death. [2] But soon it was time for the Jewish Festival of Shelters, [3] and Jesus' brothers said to him, "Leave here and go to Judea, where your followers can see your miracles! [4] You can't become famous if you hide like this! If you can do such wonderful things, show yourself to the world!" [5] For even his brothers didn't believe in him.

[6] Jesus replied, "Now is not the right time for me to go, but you can go anytime. [7] The world can't hate you, but it does hate me because I accuse it of doing evil. [8] You go on. I'm not going to this festival, because my time has not yet come." [9] After saying these things, Jesus remained in Galilee.

Jesus Teaches Openly at the Temple
[10] But after his brothers left for the festival, Jesus also went, though secretly, staying out of public view. [11] The Jewish leaders tried to find him at the festival and kept asking if anyone had seen him. [12] There was a lot of grumbling about him among the crowds. Some argued, "He's a good man," but others said, "He's nothing but a fraud who deceives the people." [13] But no one had the courage to speak favorably about him in public, for they were afraid of getting in trouble with the Jewish leaders.

[14] Then, midway through the festival, Jesus went up to the Temple and began to teach. [15] The people were surprised when they heard him. "How does he know so much when he hasn't been trained?" they asked.

[16] So Jesus told them, "My message is not my own; it comes from God who sent me. [17] Anyone who wants to do the will of God will know whether my teaching is from God or is merely my own. [18] Those who speak for themselves want glory only for themselves, but a person who seeks to honor the one who sent him speaks truth, not lies. [19] Moses gave you the law, but none of you obeys it! In fact, you are trying to kill me."

[20] The crowd replied, "You're demon possessed! Who's trying to kill you?"

[21] Jesus replied, "I did one miracle on the Sabbath, and you were amazed. [22] But you work on the Sabbath, too, when you obey Moses' law of circumcision. (Actually, this tradition of circumcision began with the

patriarchs, long before the law of Moses.) ²³ For if the correct time for circumcising your son falls on the Sabbath, you go ahead and do it so as not to break the law of Moses. So why should you be angry with me for healing a man on the Sabbath? ²⁴ Look beneath the surface so you can judge correctly."

Is Jesus the Messiah?

²⁵ Some of the people who lived in Jerusalem started to ask each other, "Isn't this the man they are trying to kill? ²⁶ But here he is, speaking in public, and they say nothing to him. Could our leaders possibly believe that he is the Messiah? ²⁷ But how could he be? For we know where this man comes from. When the Messiah comes, he will simply appear; no one will know where he comes from."

²⁸ While Jesus was teaching in the Temple, he called out, "Yes, you know me, and you know where I come from. But I'm not here on my own. The one who sent me is true, and you don't know him. ²⁹ But I know him because I come from him, and he sent me to you." ³⁰ Then the leaders tried to arrest him; but no one laid a hand on him, because his time had not yet come.

³¹ Many among the crowds at the Temple believed in him. "After all," they said, "would you expect the Messiah to do more miraculous signs than this man has done?"

³² When the Pharisees heard that the crowds were whispering such things, they and the leading priests sent Temple guards to arrest Jesus. ³³ But Jesus told them, "I will be with you only a little longer. Then I will return to the one who sent me. ³⁴ You will search for me but not find me. And you cannot go where I am going."

³⁵ The Jewish leaders were puzzled by this statement. "Where is he planning to go?" they asked. "Is he thinking of leaving the country and going to the Jews in other lands? Maybe he will even teach the Greeks! ³⁶ What does he mean when he says, 'You will search for me but not find me,' and 'You cannot go where I am going'?"

Jesus Promises Living Water

³⁷ On the last day, the climax of the festival, Jesus stood and shouted to the crowds, "Anyone who is thirsty may come to me! ³⁸ Anyone who believes in me may come and drink! For the Scriptures declare, 'Rivers of living water will flow from his heart.' " ³⁹ (When he said "living water," he was speaking of the Spirit, who would be given to everyone believing in him. But the Spirit had not yet been given, because Jesus had not yet entered into his glory.)

Division and Unbelief

[40] When the crowds heard him say this, some of them declared, "Surely this man is the Prophet we've been expecting." [41] Others said, "He is the Messiah." Still others said, "But he can't be! Will the Messiah come from Galilee? [42] For the Scriptures clearly state that the Messiah will be born of the royal line of David, in Bethlehem, the village where King David was born." [43] So the crowd was divided about him. [44] Some even wanted him arrested, but no one laid a hand on him.

[45] When the Temple guards returned without having arrested Jesus, the leading priests and Pharisees demanded, "Why didn't you bring him in?"

[46] "We have never heard anyone speak like this!" the guards responded.

[47] "Have you been led astray, too?" the Pharisees mocked. [48] "Is there a single one of us rulers or Pharisees who believes in him? [49] This foolish crowd follows him, but they are ignorant of the law. God's curse is on them!"

[50] Then Nicodemus, the leader who had met with Jesus earlier, spoke up. [51] "Is it legal to convict a man before he is given a hearing?" he asked.

[52] They replied, "Are you from Galilee, too? Search the Scriptures and see for yourself—no prophet ever comes from Galilee!"

[*The most ancient Greek manuscripts do not include John 7:53–8:11.*]

[53] Then the meeting broke up, and everybody went home.

Chapter 8

A Woman Caught in Adultery

Jesus returned to the Mount of Olives, [2] but early the next morning he was back again at the Temple. A crowd soon gathered, and he sat down and taught them. [3] As he was speaking, the teachers of religious law and the Pharisees brought a woman who had been caught in the act of adultery. They put her in front of the crowd.

[4] "Teacher," they said to Jesus, "this woman was caught in the act of adultery. [5] The law of Moses says to stone her. What do you say?"

[6] They were trying to trap him into saying something they could use against him, but Jesus stooped down and wrote in the dust with his finger. [7] They kept demanding an answer, so he stood up again and said, "All right, but let the one who has never sinned throw the first stone!" [8] Then he stooped down again and wrote in the dust.

[9] When the accusers heard this, they slipped away one by one, beginning with the oldest, until only Jesus was left in the middle of the crowd with the woman. [10] Then Jesus stood up again and said to the woman, "Where are your accusers? Didn't even one of them condemn you?"

[11] "No, Lord," she said.

And Jesus said, "Neither do I. Go and sin no more."

Jesus, the Light of the World

[12] Jesus spoke to the people once more and said, "I am the light of the world. If you follow me, you won't have to walk in darkness, because you will have the light that leads to life."

[13] The Pharisees replied, "You are making those claims about yourself! Such testimony is not valid."

[14] Jesus told them, "These claims are valid even though I make them about myself. For I know where I came from and where I am going, but you don't know this about me. [15] You judge me by human standards, but I do not judge anyone. [16] And if I did, my judgment would be correct in every respect because I am not alone. The Father who sent me is with me. [17] Your own law says that if two people agree about something, their witness is accepted as fact. [18] I am one witness, and my Father who sent me is the other."

[19] "Where is your father?" they asked.

Jesus answered, "Since you don't know who I am, you don't know who my Father is. If you knew me, you would also know my Father." [20] Jesus made these statements while he was teaching in the section of the Temple known as the Treasury. But he was not arrested, because his time had not yet come.

The Unbelieving People Warned

[21] Later Jesus said to them again, "I am going away. You will search for me but will die in your sin. You cannot come where I am going."

[22] The people asked, "Is he planning to commit suicide? What does he mean, 'You cannot come where I am going'?"

[23] Jesus continued, "You are from below; I am from above. You belong to this world; I do not. [24] That is why I said that you will die in your sins; for unless you believe that I AM who I claim to be, you will die in your sins."

[25] "Who are you?" they demanded.

Jesus replied, "The one I have always claimed to be. [26] I have much to say about you and much to condemn, but I won't. For I say only what I have heard from the one who sent me, and he is completely truthful." ²⁷ But they still didn't understand that he was talking about his Father.

²⁸ So Jesus said, "When you have lifted up the Son of Man on the cross, then you will understand that I AM he. I do nothing on my own but say only what the Father taught me. ²⁹ And the one who sent me is with me—he has not deserted me. For I always do what pleases him." ³⁰ Then many who heard him say these things believed in him.

Jesus and Abraham

³¹ Jesus said to the people who believed in him, "You are truly my disciples if you remain faithful to my teachings. ³² And you will know the truth, and the truth will set you free."

³³ "But we are descendants of Abraham," they said. "We have never been slaves to anyone. What do you mean, 'You will be set free'?"

³⁴ Jesus replied, "I tell you the truth, everyone who sins is a slave of sin. ³⁵ A slave is not a permanent member of the family, but a son is part of the family forever. ³⁶ So if the Son sets you free, you are truly free. ³⁷ Yes, I realize that you are descendants of Abraham. And yet some of you are trying to kill me because there's no room in your hearts for my message. ³⁸ I am telling you what I saw when I was with my Father. But you are following the advice of your father."

³⁹ "Our father is Abraham!" they declared.

"No," Jesus replied, "for if you were really the children of Abraham, you would follow his example. ⁴⁰ Instead, you are trying to kill me because I told you the truth, which I heard from God. Abraham never did such a thing. ⁴¹ No, you are imitating your real father."

They replied, "We aren't illegitimate children! God himself is our true Father."

⁴² Jesus told them, "If God were your Father, you would love me, because I have come to you from God. I am not here on my own, but he sent me. ⁴³ Why can't you understand what I am saying? It's because you can't even hear me! ⁴⁴ For you are the children of your father the devil, and you love to do the evil things he does. He was a murderer from the beginning. He has always hated the truth, because there is no truth in him. When he lies, it is consistent with his character; for he is a liar and the father of lies. ⁴⁵ So when I tell the truth, you just naturally don't believe me! ⁴⁶ Which of you can truthfully accuse me of sin? And since I am telling you the truth, why don't you believe me? ⁴⁷ Anyone who belongs to God listens gladly to the words of

God. But you don't listen because you don't belong to God."

⁴⁸ The people retorted, "You Samaritan devil! Didn't we say all along that you were possessed by a demon?"

⁴⁹ "No," Jesus said, "I have no demon in me. For I honor my Father—and you dishonor me. ⁵⁰ And though I have no wish to glorify myself, God is going to glorify me. He is the true judge. ⁵¹ I tell you the truth, anyone who obeys my teaching will never die!"

⁵² The people said, "Now we know you are possessed by a demon. Even Abraham and the prophets died, but you say, 'Anyone who obeys my teaching will never die!' ⁵³ Are you greater than our father Abraham? He died, and so did the prophets. Who do you think you are?"

⁵⁴ Jesus answered, "If I want glory for myself, it doesn't count. But it is my Father who will glorify me. You say, 'He is our God,' ⁵⁵ but you don't even know him. I know him. If I said otherwise, I would be as great a liar as you! But I do know him and obey him. ⁵⁶ Your father Abraham rejoiced as he looked forward to my coming. He saw it and was glad."

⁵⁷ The people said, "You aren't even fifty years old. How can you say you have seen Abraham?"

⁵⁸ Jesus answered, "I tell you the truth, before Abraham was even born, I AM!" ⁵⁹ At that point they picked up stones to throw at him. But Jesus was hidden from them and left the Temple.

Chapter 9

Jesus Heals a Man Born Blind

As Jesus was walking along, he saw a man who had been blind from birth. ² "Rabbi," his disciples asked him, "why was this man born blind? Was it because of his own sins or his parents' sins?"

³ "It was not because of his sins or his parents' sins," Jesus answered. "This happened so the power of God could be seen in him. ⁴ We must quickly carry out the tasks assigned us by the one who sent us. The night is coming, and then no one can work. ⁵ But while I am here in the world, I am the light of the world."

⁶ Then he spit on the ground, made mud with the saliva, and spread the mud over the blind man's eyes. ⁷ He told him, "Go wash yourself in the pool of Siloam" (Siloam means "sent"). So the man went and washed and came back seeing!

⁸ His neighbors and others who knew him as a blind beggar asked each other, "Isn't this the man who used to sit and beg?" ⁹ Some said he was, and others said, "No, he just looks like him!"

But the beggar kept saying, "Yes, I am the same one!"

¹⁰ They asked, "Who healed you? What happened?"

¹¹ He told them, "The man they call Jesus made mud and spread it over my eyes and told me, 'Go to the pool of Siloam and wash yourself.' So I went and washed, and now I can see!"

¹² "Where is he now?" they asked.

"I don't know," he replied.

¹³ Then they took the man who had been blind to the Pharisees, ¹⁴ because it was on the Sabbath that Jesus had made the mud and healed him. ¹⁵ The Pharisees asked the man all about it. So he told them, "He put the mud over my eyes, and when I washed it away, I could see!"

¹⁶ Some of the Pharisees said, "This man Jesus is not from God, for he is working on the Sabbath." Others said, "But how could an ordinary sinner do such miraculous signs?" So there was a deep division of opinion among them.

¹⁷ Then the Pharisees again questioned the man who had been blind and demanded, "What's your opinion about this man who healed you?"

The man replied, "I think he must be a prophet."

¹⁸ The Jewish leaders still refused to believe the man had been blind and could now see, so they called in his parents. ¹⁹ They asked them, "Is this your son? Was he born blind? If so, how can he now see?"

²⁰ His parents replied, "We know this is our son and that he was born blind, ²¹ but we don't know how he can see or who healed him. Ask him. He is old enough to speak for himself." ²² His parents said this because they were afraid of the Jewish leaders, who had announced that anyone saying Jesus was the Messiah would be expelled from the synagogue. ²³ That's why they said, "He is old enough. Ask him."

²⁴ So for the second time they called in the man who had been blind and told him, "God should get the glory for this, because we know this man Jesus is a sinner."

²⁵ "I don't know whether he is a sinner," the man replied. "But I know this: I was blind, and now I can see!"

²⁶ "But what did he do?" they asked. "How did he heal you?"

²⁷ "Look!" the man exclaimed. "I told you once. Didn't you listen? Why do you want to hear it again? Do you want to become his disciples, too?"

²⁸ Then they cursed him and said, "You are his disciple, but we are disciples of Moses! ²⁹ We know God spoke to Moses, but we don't even know where this man comes from."

³⁰ "Why, that's very strange!" the man replied. "He healed my eyes, and yet you don't know where he comes from? ³¹ We know that God doesn't listen to sinners, but he is ready to hear those who worship him and do his will. ³² Ever since the world began, no one has been able to open the eyes of someone born blind. ³³ If this man were not from God, he couldn't have done it."

³⁴ "You were born a total sinner!" they answered. "Are you trying to teach us?" And they threw him out of the synagogue.

Spiritual Blindness

³⁵ When Jesus heard what had happened, he found the man and asked, "Do you believe in the Son of Man?"

³⁶ The man answered, "Who is he, sir? I want to believe in him."

³⁷ "You have seen him," Jesus said, "and he is speaking to you!"

³⁸ "Yes, Lord, I believe!" the man said. And he worshiped Jesus.

³⁹ Then Jesus told him, "I entered this world to render judgment—to give sight to the blind and to show those who think they see that they are blind."

⁴⁰ Some Pharisees who were standing nearby heard him and asked, "Are you saying we're blind?"

⁴¹ "If you were blind, you wouldn't be guilty," Jesus replied. "But you remain guilty because you claim you can see.

Chapter 10

The Good Shepherd and His Sheep

"I tell you the truth, anyone who sneaks over the wall of a sheepfold, rather than going through the gate, must surely be a thief and a robber! ² But the one who enters through the gate is the shepherd of the sheep. ³ The gatekeeper opens the gate for him, and the sheep recognize his voice and come to him. He calls his own sheep by name and leads them out. ⁴ After he has gathered his own flock, he walks ahead of them, and they follow him because they know his voice. ⁵ They won't follow a stranger; they will run from him because they don't know his voice."

⁶ Those who heard Jesus use this illustration didn't understand what he meant, ⁷ so he explained it to them: "I tell you the truth, I am the gate for the

sheep. [8] All who came before me were thieves and robbers. But the true sheep did not listen to them. [9] Yes, I am the gate. Those who come in through me will be saved. They will come and go freely and will find good pastures. [10] The thief's purpose is to steal and kill and destroy. My purpose is to give them a rich and satisfying life.

[11] "I am the good shepherd. The good shepherd sacrifices his life for the sheep. [12] A hired hand will run when he sees a wolf coming. He will abandon the sheep because they don't belong to him and he isn't their shepherd. And so the wolf attacks them and scatters the flock. [13] The hired hand runs away because he's working only for the money and doesn't really care about the sheep.

[14] "I am the good shepherd; I know my own sheep, and they know me, [15] just as my Father knows me and I know the Father. So I sacrifice my life for the sheep. [16] I have other sheep, too, that are not in this sheepfold. I must bring them also. They will listen to my voice, and there will be one flock with one shepherd.

[17] "The Father loves me because I sacrifice my life so I may take it back again. [18] No one can take my life from me. I sacrifice it voluntarily. For I have the authority to lay it down when I want to and also to take it up again. For this is what my Father has commanded."

[19] When he said these things, the people were again divided in their opinions about him. [20] Some said, "He's demon possessed and out of his mind. Why listen to a man like that?" [21] Others said, "This doesn't sound like a man possessed by a demon! Can a demon open the eyes of the blind?"

Jesus Claims to Be the Son of God

[22] It was now winter, and Jesus was in Jerusalem at the time of Hanukkah, the Festival of Dedication. [23] He was in the Temple, walking through the section known as Solomon's Colonnade. [24] The people surrounded him and asked, "How long are you going to keep us in suspense? If you are the Messiah, tell us plainly."

[25] Jesus replied, "I have already told you, and you don't believe me. The proof is the work I do in my Father's name. [26] But you don't believe me because you are not my sheep. [27] My sheep listen to my voice; I know them, and they follow me. [28] I give them eternal life, and they will never perish. No one can snatch them away from me, [29] for my Father has given them to me, and he is more powerful than anyone else. No one can snatch them from the Father's hand. [30] The Father and I are one."

³¹ Once again the people picked up stones to kill him. ³² Jesus said, "At my Father's direction I have done many good works. For which one are you going to stone me?"

³³ They replied, "We're stoning you not for any good work, but for blasphemy! You, a mere man, claim to be God."

³⁴ Jesus replied, "It is written in your own Scriptures that God said to certain leaders of the people, 'I say, you are gods!' ³⁵ And you know that the Scriptures cannot be altered. So if those people who received God's message were called 'gods,' ³⁶ why do you call it blasphemy when I say, 'I am the Son of God'? After all, the Father set me apart and sent me into the world. ³⁷ Don't believe me unless I carry out my Father's work. ³⁸ But if I do his work, believe in the evidence of the miraculous works I have done, even if you don't believe me. Then you will know and understand that the Father is in me, and I am in the Father."

³⁹ Once again they tried to arrest him, but he got away and left them. ⁴⁰ He went beyond the Jordan River near the place where John was first baptizing and stayed there awhile. ⁴¹ And many followed him. "John didn't perform miraculous signs," they remarked to one another, "but everything he said about this man has come true." ⁴² And many who were there believed in Jesus.

Chapter 11

The Raising of Lazarus

A man named Lazarus was sick. He lived in Bethany with his sisters, Mary and Martha. ² This is the Mary who later poured the expensive perfume on the Lord's feet and wiped them with her hair. Her brother, Lazarus, was sick. ³ So the two sisters sent a message to Jesus telling him, "Lord, your dear friend is very sick."

⁴ But when Jesus heard about it he said, "Lazarus's sickness will not end in death. No, it happened for the glory of God so that the Son of God will receive glory from this." ⁵ So although Jesus loved Martha, Mary, and Lazarus, ⁶ he stayed where he was for the next two days. ⁷ Finally, he said to his disciples, "Let's go back to Judea."

⁸ But his disciples objected. "Rabbi," they said, "only a few days ago the people in Judea were trying to stone you. Are you going there again?"

⁹ Jesus replied, "There are twelve hours of daylight every day. During the day people can walk safely. They can see because they have the light of this

world. ¹⁰ But at night there is danger of stumbling because they have no light." ¹¹ Then he said, "Our friend Lazarus has fallen asleep, but now I will go and wake him up."

¹² The disciples said, "Lord, if he is sleeping, he will soon get better!" ¹³ They thought Jesus meant Lazarus was simply sleeping, but Jesus meant Lazarus had died.

¹⁴ So he told them plainly, "Lazarus is dead. ¹⁵ And for your sakes, I'm glad I wasn't there, for now you will really believe. Come, let's go see him."

¹⁶ Thomas, nicknamed the Twin, said to his fellow disciples, "Let's go, too—and die with Jesus."

¹⁷ When Jesus arrived at Bethany, he was told that Lazarus had already been in his grave for four days. ¹⁸ Bethany was only a few miles down the road from Jerusalem, ¹⁹ and many of the people had come to console Martha and Mary in their loss. ²⁰ When Martha got word that Jesus was coming, she went to meet him. But Mary stayed in the house. ²¹ Martha said to Jesus, "Lord, if only you had been here, my brother would not have died. ²² But even now I know that God will give you whatever you ask."

²³ Jesus told her, "Your brother will rise again."

²⁴ "Yes," Martha said, "he will rise when everyone else rises, at the last day."

²⁵ Jesus told her, "I am the resurrection and the life. Anyone who believes in me will live, even after dying. ²⁶ Everyone who lives in me and believes in me will never ever die. Do you believe this, Martha?"

²⁷ "Yes, Lord," she told him. "I have always believed you are the Messiah, the Son of God, the one who has come into the world from God." ²⁸ Then she returned to Mary. She called Mary aside from the mourners and told her, "The Teacher is here and wants to see you." ²⁹ So Mary immediately went to him.

³⁰ Jesus had stayed outside the village, at the place where Martha met him. ³¹ When the people who were at the house consoling Mary saw her leave so hastily, they assumed she was going to Lazarus's grave to weep. So they followed her there. ³² When Mary arrived and saw Jesus, she fell at his feet and said, "Lord, if only you had been here, my brother would not have died."

³³ When Jesus saw her weeping and saw the other people wailing with her, a deep anger welled up within him, and he was deeply troubled. ³⁴ "Where have you put him?" he asked them.

They told him, "Lord, come and see." ³⁵ Then Jesus wept. ³⁶ The people who were standing nearby said, "See how much he loved him!" ³⁷ But some said, "This man healed a blind man. Couldn't he have kept Lazarus from dying?"

[38] Jesus was still angry as he arrived at the tomb, a cave with a stone rolled across its entrance. [39] "Roll the stone aside," Jesus told them.

But Martha, the dead man's sister, protested, "Lord, he has been dead for four days. The smell will be terrible."

[40] Jesus responded, "Didn't I tell you that you would see God's glory if you believe?" [41] So they rolled the stone aside. Then Jesus looked up to heaven and said, "Father, thank you for hearing me. [42] You always hear me, but I said it out loud for the sake of all these people standing here, so that they will believe you sent me." [43] Then Jesus shouted, "Lazarus, come out!" [44] And the dead man came out, his hands and feet bound in grave clothes, his face wrapped in a head cloth. Jesus told them, "Unwrap him and let him go!"

The Plot to Kill Jesus

[45] Many of the people who were with Mary believed in Jesus when they saw this happen. [46] But some went to the Pharisees and told them what Jesus had done. [47] Then the leading priests and Pharisees called the high council together. "What are we going to do?" they asked each other. "This man certainly performs many miraculous signs. [48] If we allow him to go on like this, soon everyone will believe in him. Then the Roman army will come and destroy both our Temple and our nation."

[49] Caiaphas, who was high priest at that time, said, "You don't know what you're talking about! [50] You don't realize that it's better for you that one man should die for the people than for the whole nation to be destroyed."

[51] He did not say this on his own; as high priest at that time he was led to prophesy that Jesus would die for the entire nation. [52] And not only for that nation, but to bring together and unite all the children of God scattered around the world.

[53] So from that time on, the Jewish leaders began to plot Jesus' death. [54] As a result, Jesus stopped his public ministry among the people and left Jerusalem. He went to a place near the wilderness, to the village of Ephraim, and stayed there with his disciples.

[55] It was now almost time for the Jewish Passover celebration, and many people from all over the country arrived in Jerusalem several days early so they could go through the purification ceremony before Passover began. [56] They kept looking for Jesus, but as they stood around in the Temple, they said to each other, "What do you think? He won't come for Passover, will

he?" [57] Meanwhile, the leading priests and Pharisees had publicly ordered that anyone seeing Jesus must report it immediately so they could arrest him.

Chapter 12

Jesus Anointed at Bethany

Six days before the Passover celebration began, Jesus arrived in Bethany, the home of Lazarus—the man he had raised from the dead. [2] A dinner was prepared in Jesus' honor. Martha served, and Lazarus was among those who ate with him. [3] Then Mary took a twelve-ounce jar of expensive perfume made from essence of nard, and she anointed Jesus' feet with it, wiping his feet with her hair. The house was filled with the fragrance.

[4] But Judas Iscariot, the disciple who would soon betray him, said, [5] "That perfume was worth a year's wages. It should have been sold and the money given to the poor." [6] Not that he cared for the poor—he was a thief, and since he was in charge of the disciples' money, he often stole some for himself.

[7] Jesus replied, "Leave her alone. She did this in preparation for my burial. [8] You will always have the poor among you, but you will not always have me."

[9] When all the people heard of Jesus' arrival, they flocked to see him and also to see Lazarus, the man Jesus had raised from the dead. [10] Then the leading priests decided to kill Lazarus, too, [11] for it was because of him that many of the people had deserted them and believed in Jesus.

Jesus' Triumphant Entry

[12] The next day, the news that Jesus was on the way to Jerusalem swept through the city. A large crowd of Passover visitors [13] took palm branches and went down the road to meet him. They shouted,

> "Praise God!
> Blessings on the one who comes in the name of the LORD!
> Hail to the King of Israel!"

[14] Jesus found a young donkey and rode on it, fulfilling the prophecy that said:

> [15] "Don't be afraid, people of Jerusalem.
> Look, your King is coming,
>   riding on a donkey's colt."

[16] His disciples didn't understand at the time that this was a fulfillment of prophecy. But after Jesus entered into his glory, they remembered what had happened and realized that these things had been written about him.

[17] Many in the crowd had seen Jesus call Lazarus from the tomb, raising him from the dead, and they were telling others about it. [18] That was the reason so many went out to meet him—because they had heard about this miraculous sign. [19] Then the Pharisees said to each other, "There's nothing we can do. Look, everyone has gone after him!"

Jesus Predicts His Death

[20] Some Greeks who had come to Jerusalem for the Passover celebration [21] paid a visit to Philip, who was from Bethsaida in Galilee. They said, "Sir, we want to meet Jesus." [22] Philip told Andrew about it, and they went together to ask Jesus.

[23] Jesus replied, "Now the time has come for the Son of Man to enter into his glory. [24] I tell you the truth, unless a kernel of wheat is planted in the soil and dies, it remains alone. But its death will produce many new kernels—a plentiful harvest of new lives. [25] Those who love their life in this world will lose it. Those who care nothing for their life in this world will keep it for eternity. [26] Anyone who wants to be my disciple must follow me, because my servants must be where I am. And the Father will honor anyone who serves me.

[27] "Now my soul is deeply troubled. Should I pray, 'Father, save me from this hour'? But this is the very reason I came! [28] Father, bring glory to your name."

Then a voice spoke from heaven, saying, "I have already brought glory to my name, and I will do so again." [29] When the crowd heard the voice, some thought it was thunder, while others declared an angel had spoken to him.

[30] Then Jesus told them, "The voice was for your benefit, not mine. [31] The time for judging this world has come, when Satan, the ruler of this world, will be cast out. [32] And when I am lifted up from the earth, I will draw everyone to myself." [33] He said this to indicate how he was going to die.

[34] The crowd responded, "We understood from Scripture that the Messiah would live forever. How can you say the Son of Man will die? Just who is this Son of Man, anyway?"

[35] Jesus replied, "My light will shine for you just a little longer. Walk in the light while you can, so the darkness will not overtake you. Those who walk in the darkness cannot see where they are going. [36] Put your trust in the

light while there is still time; then you will become children of the light."

After saying these things, Jesus went away and was hidden from them.

The Unbelief of the People

[37] But despite all the miraculous signs Jesus had done, most of the people still did not believe in him. [38] This is exactly what Isaiah the prophet had predicted:

> "LORD, who has believed our message?
>> To whom has the LORD revealed his powerful arm?"

[39] But the people couldn't believe, for as Isaiah also said,

> [40] "The Lord has blinded their eyes
>> and hardened their hearts—
> so that their eyes cannot see,
>> and their hearts cannot understand,
> and they cannot turn to me
>> and have me heal them."

[41] Isaiah was referring to Jesus when he said this, because he saw the future and spoke of the Messiah's glory. [42] Many people did believe in him, however, including some of the Jewish leaders. But they wouldn't admit it for fear that the Pharisees would expel them from the synagogue. [43] For they loved human praise more than the praise of God.

[44] Jesus shouted to the crowds, "If you trust me, you are trusting not only me, but also God who sent me. [45] For when you see me, you are seeing the one who sent me. [46] I have come as a light to shine in this dark world, so that all who put their trust in me will no longer remain in the dark. [47] I will not judge those who hear me but don't obey me, for I have come to save the world and not to judge it. [48] But all who reject me and my message will be judged on the day of judgment by the truth I have spoken. [49] I don't speak on my own authority. The Father who sent me has commanded me what to say and how to say it. [50] And I know his commands lead to eternal life; so I say whatever the Father tells me to say."

Chapter 13

Jesus Washes His Disciples' Feet

Before the Passover celebration, Jesus knew that his hour had come to leave this world and return to his Father. He had loved his disciples during his ministry on earth, and now he loved them to the very end. [2] It was time for supper, and the devil had already prompted Judas, son of Simon Iscariot, to betray Jesus. [3] Jesus knew that the Father had given him authority over everything and that he had come from God and would return to God. [4] So he got up from the table, took off his robe, wrapped a towel around his waist, [5] and poured water into a basin. Then he began to wash the disciples' feet, drying them with the towel he had around him.

[6] When Jesus came to Simon Peter, Peter said to him, "Lord, are you going to wash my feet?"

[7] Jesus replied, "You don't understand now what I am doing, but someday you will."

[8] "No," Peter protested, "You will never ever wash my feet!"

Jesus replied, "Unless I wash you, you won't belong to me."

[9] Simon Peter exclaimed: "Then wash my hands and head as well, Lord, not just my feet!"

[10] Jesus replied, "A person who has bathed all over does not need to wash, except for the feet, to be entirely clean. And you disciples are clean, but not all of you." [11] For Jesus knew who would betray him. That is what he meant when he said, "Not all of you are clean."

[12] After washing their feet, he put on his robe again and sat down and asked, "Do you understand what I was doing? [13] You call me 'Teacher' and 'Lord,' and you are right, because that's what I am. [14] And since I, your Lord and Teacher, have washed your feet, you ought to wash each other's feet. [15] I have given you an example to follow. Do as I have done to you. [16] I tell you the truth, slaves are not greater than their master. Nor is the messenger more important than the one who sends the message. [17] Now that you know these things, God will bless you for doing them.

Jesus Predicts His Betrayal

[18] "I am not saying these things to all of you; I know the ones I have chosen. But this fulfills the Scripture that says, 'The one who eats my food has turned against me.' [19] I tell you this beforehand, so that when it happens you will believe that I AM the Messiah. [20] I tell you the truth, anyone who welcomes my messenger is welcoming me, and anyone who welcomes me is welcoming the Father who sent me."

[21] Now Jesus was deeply troubled, and he exclaimed, "I tell you the truth,

one of you will betray me!"

²² The disciples looked at each other, wondering whom he could mean.
²³ The disciple Jesus loved was sitting next to Jesus at the table. ²⁴ Simon Peter motioned to him to ask, "Who's he talking about?" ²⁵ So that disciple leaned over to Jesus and asked, "Lord, who is it?"

²⁶ Jesus responded, "It is the one to whom I give the bread I dip in the bowl." And when he had dipped it, he gave it to Judas, son of Simon Iscariot. ²⁷ When Judas had eaten the bread, Satan entered into him. Then Jesus told him, "Hurry and do what you're going to do." ²⁸ None of the others at the table knew what Jesus meant. ²⁹ Since Judas was their treasurer, some thought Jesus was telling him to go and pay for the food or to give some money to the poor. ³⁰ So Judas left at once, going out into the night.

Jesus Predicts Peter's Denial

³¹ As soon as Judas left the room, Jesus said, "The time has come for the Son of Man to enter into his glory, and God will be glorified because of him. ³² And since God receives glory because of the Son, he will soon give glory to the Son. ³³ Dear children, I will be with you only a little longer. And as I told the Jewish leaders, you will search for me, but you can't come where I am going. ³⁴ So now I am giving you a new commandment: Love each other. Just as I have loved you, you should love each other. ³⁵ Your love for one another will prove to the world that you are my disciples."

³⁶ Simon Peter asked, "Lord, where are you going?"

And Jesus replied, "You can't go with me now, but you will follow me later."

³⁷ "But why can't I come now, Lord?" he asked. "I'm ready to die for you."

³⁸ Jesus answered, "Die for me? I tell you the truth, Peter—before the rooster crows tomorrow morning, you will deny three times that you even know me.

Chapter 14

Jesus, the Way to the Father

"Don't let your hearts be troubled. Trust in God, and trust also in me. ² There is more than enough room in my Father's home. If this were not so, would I have told you that I am going to prepare a place for you? ³ When everything is ready, I will come and get you, so that you will always be with me where I am. [4] And you know the way to where I am going."

[5] "No, we don't know, Lord," Thomas said. "We have no idea where you are going, so how can we know the way?"

[6] Jesus told him, "I am the way, the truth, and the life. No one can come to the Father except through me. [7] If you had really known me, you would know who my Father is. From now on, you do know him and have seen him!"

[8] Philip said, "Lord, show us the Father, and we will be satisfied."

[9] Jesus replied, "Have I been with you all this time, Philip, and yet you still don't know who I am? Anyone who has seen me has seen the Father! So why are you asking me to show him to you? [10] Don't you believe that I am in the Father and the Father is in me? The words I speak are not my own, but my Father who lives in me does his work through me. [11] Just believe that I am in the Father and the Father is in me. Or at least believe because of the work you have seen me do.

[12] "I tell you the truth, anyone who believes in me will do the same works I have done, and even greater works, because I am going to be with the Father. [13] You can ask for anything in my name, and I will do it, so that the Son can bring glory to the Father. [14] Yes, ask me for anything in my name, and I will do it!

Jesus Promises the Holy Spirit

[15] "If you love me, obey my commandments. [16] And I will ask the Father, and he will give you another Advocate, who will never leave you. [17] He is the Holy Spirit, who leads into all truth. The world cannot receive him, because it isn't looking for him and doesn't recognize him. But you know him, because he lives with you now and later will be in you. [18] No, I will not abandon you as orphans—I will come to you. [19] Soon the world will no longer see me, but you will see me. Since I live, you also will live. [20] When I am raised to life again, you will know that I am in my Father, and you are in me, and I am in you. [21] Those who accept my commandments and obey them are the ones who love me. And because they love me, my Father will love them. And I will love them and reveal myself to each of them."

[22] Judas (not Judas Iscariot, but the other disciple with that name) said to him, "Lord, why are you going to reveal yourself only to us and not to the world at large?"

[23] Jesus replied, "All who love me will do what I say. My Father will love them, and we will come and make our home with each of them. [24] Anyone who doesn't love me will not obey me. And remember, my words are not my

own. What I am telling you is from the Father who sent me. [25] I am telling you these things now while I am still with you. [26] But when the Father sends the Advocate as my representative—that is, the Holy Spirit—he will teach you everything and will remind you of everything I have told you.

[27] "I am leaving you with a gift—peace of mind and heart. And the peace I give is a gift the world cannot give. So don't be troubled or afraid. [28] Remember what I told you: I am going away, but I will come back to you again. If you really loved me, you would be happy that I am going to the Father, who is greater than I am. [29] I have told you these things before they happen so that when they do happen, you will believe.

[30] "I don't have much more time to talk to you, because the ruler of this world approaches. He has no power over me, [31] but I will do what the Father requires of me, so that the world will know that I love the Father. Come, let's be going.

Chapter 15

Jesus, the True Vine
"I am the true grapevine, and my Father is the gardener. [2] He cuts off every branch of mine that doesn't produce fruit, and he prunes the branches that do bear fruit so they will produce even more. [3] You have already been pruned and purified by the message I have given you. [4] Remain in me, and I will remain in you. For a branch cannot produce fruit if it is severed from the vine, and you cannot be fruitful unless you remain in me.

[5] "Yes, I am the vine; you are the branches. Those who remain in me, and I in them, will produce much fruit. For apart from me you can do nothing. [6] Anyone who does not remain in me is thrown away like a useless branch and withers. Such branches are gathered into a pile to be burned. [7] But if you remain in me and my words remain in you, you may ask for anything you want, and it will be granted! [8] When you produce much fruit, you are my true disciples. This brings great glory to my Father.

[9] "I have loved you even as the Father has loved me. Remain in my love. [10] When you obey my commandments, you remain in my love, just as I obey my Father's commandments and remain in his love. [11] I have told you these things so that you will be filled with my joy. Yes, your joy will overflow! [12] This is my commandment: Love each other in the same way I have loved you. [13] There is no greater love than to lay down one's life for one's friends.

[14] You are my friends if you do what I command. [15] I no longer call you slaves, because a master doesn't confide in his slaves. Now you are my friends, since I have told you everything the Father told me. [16] You didn't choose me. I chose you. I appointed you to go and produce lasting fruit, so that the Father will give you whatever you ask for, using my name. [17] This is my command: Love each other.

The World's Hatred

[18] "If the world hates you, remember that it hated me first. [19] The world would love you as one of its own if you belonged to it, but you are no longer part of the world. I chose you to come out of the world, so it hates you. [20] Do you remember what I told you? 'A slave is not greater than the master.' Since they persecuted me, naturally they will persecute you. And if they had listened to me, they would listen to you. [21] They will do all this to you because of me, for they have rejected the one who sent me. [22] They would not be guilty if I had not come and spoken to them. But now they have no excuse for their sin. [23] Anyone who hates me also hates my Father. [24] If I hadn't done such miraculous signs among them that no one else could do, they would not be guilty. But as it is, they have seen everything I did, yet they still hate me and my Father. [25] This fulfills what is written in their Scriptures: 'They hated me without cause.'

[26] "But I will send you the Advocate—the Spirit of truth. He will come to you from the Father and will testify all about me. [27] And you must also testify about me because you have been with me from the beginning of my ministry.

Chapter 16

"I have told you these things so that you won't abandon your faith. [2] For you will be expelled from the synagogues, and the time is coming when those who kill you will think they are doing a holy service for God. [3] This is because they have never known the Father or me. [4] Yes, I'm telling you these things now, so that when they happen, you will remember my warning. I didn't tell you earlier because I was going to be with you for a while longer.

The Work of the Holy Spirit

[5] "But now I am going away to the one who sent me, and not one of you is asking where I am going. [6] Instead, you grieve because of what I've told you. [7] But in fact, it is best for you that I go away, because if I don't, the Advocate

won't come. If I do go away, then I will send him to you. [8] And when he comes, he will convict the world of its sin, and of God's righteousness, and of the coming judgment. [9] The world's sin is that it refuses to believe in me. [10] Righteousness is available because I go to the Father, and you will see me no more. [11] Judgment will come because the ruler of this world has already been judged.

[12] "There is so much more I want to tell you, but you can't bear it now. [13] When the Spirit of truth comes, he will guide you into all truth. He will not speak on his own but will tell you what he has heard. He will tell you about the future. [14] He will bring me glory by telling you whatever he receives from me. [15] All that belongs to the Father is mine; this is why I said, 'The Spirit will tell you whatever he receives from me.'

Sadness Will Be Turned to Joy

[16] "In a little while you won't see me anymore. But a little while after that, you will see me again."

[17] Some of the disciples asked each other, "What does he mean when he says, 'In a little while you won't see me, but then you will see me,' and 'I am going to the Father'? [18] And what does he mean by 'a little while'? We don't understand."

[19] Jesus realized they wanted to ask him about it, so he said, "Are you asking yourselves what I meant? I said in a little while you won't see me, but a little while after that you will see me again. [20] I tell you the truth, you will weep and mourn over what is going to happen to me, but the world will rejoice. You will grieve, but your grief will suddenly turn to wonderful joy. [21] It will be like a woman suffering the pains of labor. When her child is born, her anguish gives way to joy because she has brought a new baby into the world. [22] So you have sorrow now, but I will see you again; then you will rejoice, and no one can rob you of that joy. [23] At that time you won't need to ask me for anything. I tell you the truth, you will ask the Father directly, and he will grant your request because you use my name. [24] You haven't done this before. Ask, using my name, and you will receive, and you will have abundant joy.

[25] "I have spoken of these matters in figures of speech, but soon I will stop speaking figuratively and will tell you plainly all about the Father. [26] Then you will ask in my name. I'm not saying I will ask the Father on your behalf, [27] for the Father himself loves you dearly because you love me and believe that I came from God. [28] Yes, I came from the Father into the world, and now

I will leave the world and return to the Father."

²⁹ Then his disciples said, "At last you are speaking plainly and not figuratively. ³⁰ Now we understand that you know everything, and there's no need to question you. From this we believe that you came from God."

³¹ Jesus asked, "Do you finally believe? ³² But the time is coming—indeed it's here now—when you will be scattered, each one going his own way, leaving me alone. Yet I am not alone because the Father is with me. ³³ I have told you all this so that you may have peace in me. Here on earth you will have many trials and sorrows. But take heart, because I have overcome the world."

Chapter 17

The Prayer of Jesus

After saying all these things, Jesus looked up to heaven and said, "Father, the hour has come. Glorify your Son so he can give glory back to you. ² For you have given him authority over everyone. He gives eternal life to each one you have given him. ³ And this is the way to have eternal life—to know you, the only true God, and Jesus Christ, the one you sent to earth. ⁴ I brought glory to you here on earth by completing the work you gave me to do. ⁵ Now, Father, bring me into the glory we shared before the world began.

⁶ "I have revealed you to the ones you gave me from this world. They were always yours. You gave them to me, and they have kept your word. ⁷ Now they know that everything I have is a gift from you, ⁸ for I have passed on to them the message you gave me. They accepted it and know that I came from you, and they believe you sent me.

⁹ "My prayer is not for the world, but for those you have given me, because they belong to you. ¹⁰ All who are mine belong to you, and you have given them to me, so they bring me glory. ¹¹ Now I am departing from the world; they are staying in this world, but I am coming to you. Holy Father, you have given me your name; now protect them by the power of your name so that they will be united just as we are. ¹² During my time here, I protected them by the power of the name you gave me. I guarded them so that not one was lost, except the one headed for destruction, as the Scriptures foretold.

¹³ "Now I am coming to you. I told them many things while I was with them in this world so they would be filled with my joy. ¹⁴ I have given them your word. And the world hates them because they do not belong to the

world, just as I do not belong to the world. [15] I'm not asking you to take them out of the world, but to keep them safe from the evil one. [16] They do not belong to this world any more than I do. [17] Make them holy by your truth; teach them your word, which is truth. [18] Just as you sent me into the world, I am sending them into the world. [19] And I give myself as a holy sacrifice for them so they can be made holy by your truth.

[20] "I am praying not only for these disciples but also for all who will ever believe in me through their message. [21] I pray that they will all be one, just as you and I are one—as you are in me, Father, and I am in you. And may they be in us so that the world will believe you sent me.

[22] "I have given them the glory you gave me, so they may be one as we are one. [23] I am in them and you are in me. May they experience such perfect unity that the world will know that you sent me and that you love them as much as you love me. [24] Father, I want these whom you have given me to be with me where I am. Then they can see all the glory you gave me because you loved me even before the world began!

[25] "O righteous Father, the world doesn't know you, but I do; and these disciples know you sent me. [26] I have revealed you to them, and I will continue to do so. Then your love for me will be in them, and I will be in them."

Chapter 18

Jesus Is Betrayed and Arrested
After saying these things, Jesus crossed the Kidron Valley with his disciples and entered a grove of olive trees. [2] Judas, the betrayer, knew this place, because Jesus had often gone there with his disciples. [3] The leading priests and Pharisees had given Judas a contingent of Roman soldiers and Temple guards to accompany him. Now with blazing torches, lanterns, and weapons, they arrived at the olive grove.

[4] Jesus fully realized all that was going to happen to him, so he stepped forward to meet them. "Who are you looking for?" he asked.

[5] "Jesus the Nazarene," they replied.

"I AM he," Jesus said. (Judas, who betrayed him, was standing with them.) [6] As Jesus said "I AM he," they all drew back and fell to the ground! [7] Once more he asked them, "Who are you looking for?"

And again they replied, "Jesus the Nazarene."

[8] "I told you that I AM he," Jesus said. "And since I am the one you want, let these others go." [9] He did this to fulfill his own statement: "I did not lose a single one of those you have given me."

[10] Then Simon Peter drew a sword and slashed off the right ear of Malchus, the high priest's slave. [11] But Jesus said to Peter, "Put your sword back into its sheath. Shall I not drink from the cup of suffering the Father has given me?"

Jesus at the High Priest's House

[12] So the soldiers, their commanding officer, and the Temple guards arrested Jesus and tied him up. [13] First they took him to Annas, the father-in-law of Caiaphas, the high priest at that time. [14] Caiaphas was the one who had told the other Jewish leaders, "It's better that one man should die for the people."

Peter's First Denial

[15] Simon Peter followed Jesus, as did another of the disciples. That other disciple was acquainted with the high priest, so he was allowed to enter the high priest's courtyard with Jesus. [16] Peter had to stay outside the gate. Then the disciple who knew the high priest spoke to the woman watching at the gate, and she let Peter in. [17] The woman asked Peter, "You're not one of that man's disciples, are you?"

"No," he said, "I am not."

[18] Because it was cold, the household servants and the guards had made a charcoal fire. They stood around it, warming themselves, and Peter stood with them, warming himself.

The High Priest Questions Jesus

[19] Inside, the high priest began asking Jesus about his followers and what he had been teaching them. [20] Jesus replied, "Everyone knows what I teach. I have preached regularly in the synagogues and the Temple, where the people gather. I have not spoken in secret. [21] Why are you asking me this question? Ask those who heard me. They know what I said."

[22] Then one of the Temple guards standing nearby slapped Jesus across the face. "Is that the way to answer the high priest?" he demanded.

[23] Jesus replied, "If I said anything wrong, you must prove it. But if I'm speaking the truth, why are you beating me?"

[24] Then Annas bound Jesus and sent him to Caiaphas, the high priest.

Peter's Second and Third Denials

^{25} Meanwhile, as Simon Peter was standing by the fire warming himself, they asked him again, "You're not one of his disciples, are you?"

He denied it, saying, "No, I am not."

^{26} But one of the household slaves of the high priest, a relative of the man whose ear Peter had cut off, asked, "Didn't I see you out there in the olive grove with Jesus?" ^{27} Again Peter denied it. And immediately a rooster crowed.

Jesus' Trial before Pilate

^{28} Jesus' trial before Caiaphas ended in the early hours of the morning. Then he was taken to the headquarters of the Roman governor. His accusers didn't go inside because it would defile them, and they wouldn't be allowed to celebrate the Passover. ^{29} So Pilate, the governor, went out to them and asked, "What is your charge against this man?"

^{30} "We wouldn't have handed him over to you if he weren't a criminal!" they retorted.

^{31} "Then take him away and judge him by your own law," Pilate told them.

"Only the Romans are permitted to execute someone," the Jewish leaders replied. ^{32} (This fulfilled Jesus' prediction about the way he would die.)

^{33} Then Pilate went back into his headquarters and called for Jesus to be brought to him. "Are you the king of the Jews?" he asked him.

^{34} Jesus replied, "Is this your own question, or did others tell you about me?"

^{35} "Am I a Jew?" Pilate retorted. "Your own people and their leading priests brought you to me for trial. Why? What have you done?"

^{36} Jesus answered, "My Kingdom is not an earthly kingdom. If it were, my followers would fight to keep me from being handed over to the Jewish leaders. But my Kingdom is not of this world."

^{37} Pilate said, "So you are a king?"

Jesus responded, "You say I am a king. Actually, I was born and came into the world to testify to the truth. All who love the truth recognize that what I say is true."

^{38} "What is truth?" Pilate asked. Then he went out again to the people and told them, "He is not guilty of any crime. ^{39} But you have a custom of asking me to release one prisoner each year at Passover. Would you like me to release this 'King of the Jews'?"

^{40} But they shouted back, "No! Not this man. We want Barabbas!"

(Barabbas was a revolutionary.)

Chapter 19

Jesus Sentenced to Death

Then Pilate had Jesus flogged with a lead-tipped whip. [2] The soldiers wove a crown of thorns and put it on his head, and they put a purple robe on him. [3] "Hail! King of the Jews!" they mocked, as they slapped him across the face.

[4] Pilate went outside again and said to the people, "I am going to bring him out to you now, but understand clearly that I find him not guilty." [5] Then Jesus came out wearing the crown of thorns and the purple robe. And Pilate said, "Look, here is the man!"

[6] When they saw him, the leading priests and Temple guards began shouting, "Crucify him! Crucify him!"

"Take him yourselves and crucify him," Pilate said. "I find him not guilty."

[7] The Jewish leaders replied, "By our law he ought to die because he called himself the Son of God."

[8] When Pilate heard this, he was more frightened than ever. [9] He took Jesus back into the headquarters again and asked him, "Where are you from?" But Jesus gave no answer. [10] "Why don't you talk to me?" Pilate demanded. "Don't you realize that I have the power to release you or crucify you?"

[11] Then Jesus said, "You would have no power over me at all unless it were given to you from above. So the one who handed me over to you has the greater sin."

[12] Then Pilate tried to release him, but the Jewish leaders shouted, "If you release this man, you are no 'friend of Caesar.' Anyone who declares himself a king is a rebel against Caesar."

[13] When they said this, Pilate brought Jesus out to them again. Then Pilate sat down on the judgment seat on the platform that is called the Stone Pavement (in Hebrew, *Gabbatha*). [14] It was now about noon on the day of preparation for the Passover. And Pilate said to the people, "Look, here is your king!"

[15] "Away with him," they yelled. "Away with him! Crucify him!"

"What? Crucify your king?" Pilate asked.

"We have no king but Caesar," the leading priests shouted back.

[16] Then Pilate turned Jesus over to them to be crucified.

The Crucifixion

So they took Jesus away. [17] Carrying the cross by himself, he went to the place called Place of the Skull (in Hebrew, *Golgotha*). [18] There they nailed him to the cross. Two others were crucified with him, one on either side, with Jesus between them. [19] And Pilate posted a sign on the cross that read, "Jesus of Nazareth, the King of the Jews." [20] The place where Jesus was crucified was near the city, and the sign was written in Hebrew, Latin, and Greek, so that many people could read it.

[21] Then the leading priests objected and said to Pilate, "Change it from 'The King of the Jews' to 'He said, I am King of the Jews.' "

[22] Pilate replied, "No, what I have written, I have written."

[23] When the soldiers had crucified Jesus, they divided his clothes among the four of them. They also took his robe, but it was seamless, woven in one piece from top to bottom. [24] So they said, "Rather than tearing it apart, let's throw dice for it." This fulfilled the Scripture that says, "They divided my garments among themselves and threw dice for my clothing." So that is what they did.

[25] Standing near the cross were Jesus' mother, and his mother's sister, Mary (the wife of Clopas), and Mary Magdalene. [26] When Jesus saw his mother standing there beside the disciple he loved, he said to her, "Dear woman, here is your son." [27] And he said to this disciple, "Here is your mother." And from then on this disciple took her into his home.

The Death of Jesus

[28] Jesus knew that his mission was now finished, and to fulfill Scripture he said, "I am thirsty." [29] A jar of sour wine was sitting there, so they soaked a sponge in it, put it on a hyssop branch, and held it up to his lips. [30] When Jesus had tasted it, he said, "It is finished!" Then he bowed his head and released his spirit.

[31] It was the day of preparation, and the Jewish leaders didn't want the bodies hanging there the next day, which was the Sabbath (and a very special Sabbath, because it was the Passover). So they asked Pilate to hasten their deaths by ordering that their legs be broken. Then their bodies could be taken down. [32] So the soldiers came and broke the legs of the two men crucified with Jesus. [33] But when they came to Jesus, they saw that he was already dead, so they didn't break his legs. [34] One of the soldiers, however, pierced his side with a spear, and immediately blood and water flowed out. [35] (This report is from an eyewitness giving an accurate account. He speaks the truth so that

you also can believe.) [36] These things happened in fulfillment of the Scriptures that say, "Not one of his bones will be broken," [37] and "They will look on the one they pierced."

The Burial of Jesus

[38] Afterward Joseph of Arimathea, who had been a secret disciple of Jesus (because he feared the Jewish leaders), asked Pilate for permission to take down Jesus' body. When Pilate gave permission, Joseph came and took the body away. [39] With him came Nicodemus, the man who had come to Jesus at night. He brought about seventy-five pounds of perfumed ointment made from myrrh and aloes. [40] Following Jewish burial custom, they wrapped Jesus' body with the spices in long sheets of linen cloth. [41] The place of crucifixion was near a garden, where there was a new tomb, never used before. [42] And so, because it was the day of preparation for the Jewish Passover and since the tomb was close at hand, they laid Jesus there.

Chapter 20

The Resurrection

Early on Sunday morning, while it was still dark, Mary Magdalene came to the tomb and found that the stone had been rolled away from the entrance. [2] She ran and found Simon Peter and the other disciple, the one whom Jesus loved. She said, "They have taken the Lord's body out of the tomb, and we don't know where they have put him!"

[3] Peter and the other disciple started out for the tomb. [4] They were both running, but the other disciple outran Peter and reached the tomb first. [5] He stooped and looked in and saw the linen wrappings lying there, but he didn't go in. [6] Then Simon Peter arrived and went inside. He also noticed the linen wrappings lying there, [7] while the cloth that had covered Jesus' head was folded up and lying apart from the other wrappings. [8] Then the disciple who had reached the tomb first also went in, and he saw and believed—[9] for until then they still hadn't understood the Scriptures that said Jesus must rise from the dead. [10] Then they went home.

Jesus Appears to Mary Magdalene

[11] Mary was standing outside the tomb crying, and as she wept, she stooped and looked in. [12] She saw two white-robed angels, one sitting at the head and the other at the foot of the place where the body of Jesus had been lying.

[13] "Dear woman, why are you crying?" the angels asked her.

"Because they have taken away my Lord," she replied, "and I don't know where they have put him."

[14] She turned to leave and saw someone standing there. It was Jesus, but she didn't recognize him. [15] "Dear woman, why are you crying?" Jesus asked her. "Who are you looking for?"

She thought he was the gardener. "Sir," she said, "if you have taken him away, tell me where you have put him, and I will go and get him."

[16] "Mary!" Jesus said.

She turned to him and cried out, "Rabboni!" (which is Hebrew for "Teacher").

[17] "Don't cling to me," Jesus said, "for I haven't yet ascended to the Father. But go find my brothers and tell them, 'I am ascending to my Father and your Father, to my God and your God.' "

[18] Mary Magdalene found the disciples and told them, "I have seen the Lord!" Then she gave them his message.

Jesus Appears to His Disciples

[19] That Sunday evening the disciples were meeting behind locked doors because they were afraid of the Jewish leaders. Suddenly, Jesus was standing there among them! "Peace be with you," he said. [20] As he spoke, he showed them the wounds in his hands and his side. They were filled with joy when they saw the Lord! [21] Again he said, "Peace be with you. As the Father has sent me, so I am sending you." [22] Then he breathed on them and said, "Receive the Holy Spirit. [23] If you forgive anyone's sins, they are forgiven. If you do not forgive them, they are not forgiven."

Jesus Appears to Thomas

[24] One of the twelve disciples, Thomas (nicknamed the Twin), was not with the others when Jesus came. [25] They told him, "We have seen the Lord!"

But he replied, "I won't believe it unless I see the nail wounds in his hands, put my fingers into them, and place my hand into the wound in his side."

[26] Eight days later the disciples were together again, and this time Thomas was with them. The doors were locked; but suddenly, as before, Jesus was standing among them. "Peace be with you," he said. [27] Then he said to Thomas, "Put your finger here, and look at my hands. Put your hand into the wound in my side. Don't be faithless any longer. Believe!"

²⁸ "My Lord and my God!" Thomas exclaimed.

²⁹ Then Jesus told him, "You believe because you have seen me. Blessed are those who believe without seeing me."

Purpose of the Book

³⁰ The disciples saw Jesus do many other miraculous signs in addition to the ones recorded in this book. ³¹ But these are written so that you may continue to believe that Jesus is the Messiah, the Son of God, and that by believing in him you will have life by the power of his name.

Chapter 21

Epilogue: Jesus Appears to Seven Disciples

Later, Jesus appeared again to the disciples beside the Sea of Galilee. This is how it happened. ² Several of the disciples were there—Simon Peter, Thomas (nicknamed the Twin), Nathanael from Cana in Galilee, the sons of Zebedee, and two other disciples.

³ Simon Peter said, "I'm going fishing."

"We'll come, too," they all said. So they went out in the boat, but they caught nothing all night.

⁴ At dawn Jesus was standing on the beach, but the disciples couldn't see who he was. ⁵ He called out, "Fellows, have you caught any fish?"

"No," they replied.

⁶ Then he said, "Throw out your net on the right-hand side of the boat, and you'll get some!" So they did, and they couldn't haul in the net because there were so many fish in it.

⁷ Then the disciple Jesus loved said to Peter, "It's the Lord!" When Simon Peter heard that it was the Lord, he put on his tunic (for he had stripped for work), jumped into the water, and headed to shore. ⁸ The others stayed with the boat and pulled the loaded net to the shore, for they were only about a hundred yards from shore. ⁹ When they got there, they found breakfast waiting for them—fish cooking over a charcoal fire, and some bread.

¹⁰ "Bring some of the fish you've just caught," Jesus said. ¹¹ So Simon Peter went aboard and dragged the net to the shore. There were 153 large fish, and yet the net hadn't torn.

¹² "Now come and have some breakfast!" Jesus said. None of the disciples dared to ask him, "Who are you?" They knew it was the Lord. ¹³ Then Jesus served them the bread and the fish. ¹⁴ This was the third time Jesus had

appeared to his disciples since he had been raised from the dead.

[15] After breakfast Jesus asked Simon Peter, "Simon son of John, do you love me more than these?"

"Yes, Lord," Peter replied, "you know I love you."

"Then feed my lambs," Jesus told him.

[16] Jesus repeated the question: "Simon son of John, do you love me?"

"Yes, Lord," Peter said, "you know I love you."

"Then take care of my sheep," Jesus said.

[17] A third time he asked him, "Simon son of John, do you love me?"

Peter was hurt that Jesus asked the question a third time. He said, "Lord, you know everything. You know that I love you."

Jesus said, "Then feed my sheep.

[18] "I tell you the truth, when you were young, you were able to do as you liked; you dressed yourself and went wherever you wanted to go. But when you are old, you will stretch out your hands, and others will dress you and take you where you don't want to go." [19] Jesus said this to let him know by what kind of death he would glorify God. Then Jesus told him, "Follow me."

[20] Peter turned around and saw behind them the disciple Jesus loved—the one who had leaned over to Jesus during supper and asked, "Lord, who will betray you?" [21] Peter asked Jesus, "What about him, Lord?"

[22] Jesus replied, "If I want him to remain alive until I return, what is that to you? As for you, follow me." [23] So the rumor spread among the community of believers that this disciple wouldn't die. But that isn't what Jesus said at all. He only said, "If I want him to remain alive until I return, what is that to you?"

[24] This disciple is the one who testifies to these events and has recorded them here. And we know that his account of these things is accurate.

[25] Jesus also did many other things. If they were all written down, I suppose the whole world could not contain the books that would be written.

Journal

Journal

Journal

Journal

Journal

Pastor Kenneth Sesley

Kenneth Sesley founding apostolic team leader and senior pastor of Calvary Fellowship International in Carson, CA (www.calvaryfi.com). Pastor Sesley is also the current president of the South Bay Ministers Fellowship and the founder of the RadicalCoaching.com network (an organization that provides training and resources to pastors and church leaders). Dr. Sesley's other books include 50 Days of Faith, Firstfruits, God's River of Prosperity and 35 Days of Personal Spiritual Training. Prior to entering pastoral ministry, Kenneth served as a Youth Pastor, Senior Assistant Pastor, as well as a church and conference speaker all over Southern California. Pastor Sesley is also married with three daughters and one son.

CALVARY FELLOWSHIP INTERNATIONAL

I invite you to be **my special guest this Sunday** or sometime real soon at **Calvary Fellowship International.** For more information, books or speaking requests...

You may contact us at: www.CalvaryFI.com.

Our mailing address is:

P. O. Box 5101 | Carson, CA 90749 | 310.766.6190

If someone gave you this book and you live outside of Southern California, and you need help finding a local church, please contact my church office at the above phone number or contact us at **info@calvaryfi.com.** We would be glad to help you find a great church anywhere in America.

www.ingramcontent.com/pod-product-compliance
Lightning Source LLC
Chambersburg PA
CBHW072024040426
42447CB00009B/1718